THE SUM OF OUR EXPERIENCE

Cheryl J. McCullough

BURKWOOD
Media Group

Copyright © 2020 by Cheryl J. McCullough

This is a work of fiction. All rights reserved. No part of this publication may be reproduced, distributed, or transmitted in any form or by any means, including photocopying, recording, or other electronic or mechanical methods, without the prior written permission of the publisher, except in the case of brief quotations embodied in critical reviews and certain other noncommercial uses permitted by copyright law.

For permission requests, write to the publisher, addressed "Attention: Permissions Coordinator," at the address below.

Burkwood Media Group
P O Box 1772
Albemarle. NC 28001-5704
www.burkwoodmedia.com

Printed in the United States of America

Book cover design by Sherry Simmons

sherry@twomonkeysdesign.com

www.twomonkeysdesign.com

Acknowledgements

To my family, friends and readers across the country who insisted I write this story. Especially a group of church ladies in Houston, Texas, a couple of ladies from Minneapolis, Minnesota who I vacationed with, and a group of ladies in Charlotte, North Carolina who joined me for "Tea and Talk."

You have lived with these characters as though they were your family, and friends; or even you. I am sincerely grateful for your love and support. I appreciate every compliment, word of encouragement, question and critique.

This is definitely the final installment in this series, but stay tuned, you may hear from some of these characters again.

Much love and many blessings!

Chapter 1

April stood at the door stunned. She couldn't believe her eyes. Melissa was standing there. Her mother was standing there! April thought she was looking in a mirror. The woman standing on the other side of the door had the same complexion, the same eyes, high cheekbones and smile. April didn't notice Lane standing behind her. What was different about her though, her lips looked chapped, there were spots on her face, and especially her forehead that looked like sunburns.

Lane put his drink down, walked closer and put his hand on her shoulder. April glanced back at him, didn't say anything but had a sense of comfort.

"April! How are you?" Melissa's voice was hoarse, but she sounded cheerful.

April looked at Melissa's coat. It was a very nice gray cashmere, fitted at the waist, but it was too big.

"Why are you here?" April asked forcefully.

"It's Christmas. I want to see my daughter for my last holiday."

April laughed loudly. Lane put his arm around her. He didn't know what to expect next.

Chapter 2

Jacksa Baye was exasperated when her friend and neighbor Nina opened the door. She was talking so fast, Nina finally grabbed her shoulders and shook her slightly.

"Jacksa what are you talking about?"

A few months before Jacksa was told her FBI agent fiancé, Anderson Thorn was missing and presumed dead as a result of an undercover assignment he was handling. This all happened literally days before they were to get married.

After a few weeks, his mother and sisters asked Jacksa to have a memorial service for him, so they could all have closure. She refused, not convinced Anderson was dead.

When Nina was finally able to calm Jacksa enough to understand what she was saying, Jacksa told her she received a message from Anderson's FBI handler. She had to come to the airport. She was told to bring her passport, and only essential personal items like medicine. She was also directed to get a ride to the airport, and not to tell her family she was leaving.

"I need to go now, but I couldn't leave Pepper," Jacksa told Nina. "And, will you take me to the airport? Oh my God. I am so nervous. I don't know if this means they found him or…"

Jacksa closed her eyes, and stood very still for a moment. Nina quickly redirected the conversation.

"Don't start trying to figure it out. Just get ready, I will take you, and I'll keep Pepper. Oreo will appreciate the company." Suddenly Nina had a thought. "Jacksa are you sure the person who called you is who he said he is?" Jacksa hesitated for a split second.

"Oh yes. Yes, I'm certain. He called on the phone the agent gave me and he knew the password. And that's the phone I have to bring with me. I want to leave my phone with you too."

"Okay! I'll be there in ten minutes."

"Thank you!" Jacksa said hugging Nina and leaving.

Nina got dressed, grabbed her phone and purse. "Let's go Oreo."

Jacksa was waiting, she opened the door to Nina's SUV, Pepper jumped in beside Oreo, and they headed to the airport.

As they drove, Jacksa typed into the notes on Nina's phone Anderson's sister's numbers, her brother's number and the password to her phone. "You have the key and my alarm code right?"

"Yep," Nina said.

"There's plenty of dog food."

"No worries, I'll take care of all that. Just please let me know you're okay."

"Definitely."

Nina dropped Jacksa at the airport, silently praying everything was okay. Jacksa remembered specifically what the agent told her. She headed for the ticket counter, checked in and went straight to security. Looking down at the ticket, it said San Antonio. Her heart was beating so fast she could hear it over the airport noise. She was security pre-check so it didn't take but a few minutes, and she was headed for the gate.

In the gate waiting area, a young lady approached Jacksa and introduced herself.

"Hi Jacksa, I'm Wendy Wolfe." They shook hands, and smiled at each other. "Wolf" was the password. They chatted about law school and taking the entrance exam. At the same time, Wendy was sending Jacksa texts to the phone the bureau had given her. The texts provided further instructions for the trip.

A few hours later Jacksa landed in Riviera Maya, Mexico. At that point she was puzzled. As soon as she walked off the plane there was a uniformed gentleman standing there and holding a sign that said "Wolf." She approached him. "This way to the car please."

They walked quickly. A black SUV limo sat at the curb. The man opened the back door. Jacksa climbed in; right into Anderson's arms.

Chapter 3

Kathy was numb. The doctor's words were stuck in her head. Pregnant. Pregnant? That was impossible. Sterling had used condoms and "we were very careful," she thought.

Kathy drove back to her apartment, but didn't remember how she got there. Nor did she remember taking her school bag from the car, walking through the deck and coming up the elevator. When she woke from the day dream it was getting dark. She did recall needing to pack. Her flight home was the next day for Christmas break. Sterling was meeting her at the airport, and the college Christmas party was the following night. Her parents would be at the party; her mother was on the board of trustees for DavisTown College. Her cousin Michelle would also be home for Christmas.

Kathy managed to get on her feet and then started to cry uncontrollably for several minutes. Finally gaining her composure, she realized there were missed calls from Sterling and Michelle. But she couldn't return either call. Not now.

Mindlessly, Kathy packed her things then showered and got in bed. She knew Sterling would call again, so she called him. He answered on the first ring. "Hey beautiful!" She laughed slightly. There was a peace in the sound of his voice. "Hey yourself!"

"How was your day?" He asked. He was eating something. She didn't answer his question, asking instead, "What are you eating?"

 "Sweet potato fries and a salad."

"Sounds good."

They talked for a while, and she avoided him knowing anything was wrong.
"Let me know when you land," he said as they were about to hang up.

"Will do." She replied.

"Love you!"

Her voice cracked as she responded, "I love you too."

Chapter 4

Jackson and Min were so worried about Jacksa they hadn't talked much about marriage counseling. Jackson didn't like Anderson, but he was genuinely concerned about his whereabouts. When Jacksa told them Anderson was presumed dead, he was actually devastated. He didn't say anything to Jacksa, but he told Min that was exactly why he didn't want Anderson in their daughter's life. But he had to be alive because Jackson knew Jacksa would never be the same if he wasn't.

If he could keep things on the track they were on, he and Min could work out their own troubles. Or at least that's what Jackson hoped. There was nothing good to come from them meeting with a counselor if it turned out to be her work friend, and his ex-lover. She didn't need to know about his status with Min, but more than that, Min didn't need to know her friend and co-worker was the woman who caused all this. That knowledge would surely end his marriage and most likely end her counseling career.

Chapter 5

Katherine and Lee finished dinner just as his phone rang. He stepped into his office to take the call, and she cleared the table. Knowing he would be a while, Katherine sent a text message to Sterling.

"Lee doesn't know Kathy is coming if you want her to stay with you tonight."

He didn't respond immediately.

She hoped their plan worked. Sterling told her that Kathy was remorseful about losing her virginity outside of marriage.

"Did you make her understand you love her?" Katherine had asked him.

"Yeah, you know I did. I told her that in my heart we are married."

Katherine and Sterling wanted the same thing; Kathy out of New York, back home and for Kathy and Sterling to be married. The only way to guarantee that would happen was for her to be pregnant. She just hoped his plan worked. When

Katherine suggested Sterling talk Kathy into having sex with him, neither of them considered Kathy would insist they use a condom. His idea to stick a pin hole in it was brilliant. They were together so seldom though, Sterling needed to take advantage of any opportunity to spend the night together.

Still no response from Sterling. "Oh well. I will have to wait and see what happens; if she comes here or not." Katherine left her phone on the counter, and joined Lee in the den.

The traffic at the airport was horrible. Before Sterling could park, Kathy texted to say they landed. He texted back, he would pick her up in the departures area upstairs. He saw Katherine's text. He was glad for the heads up about Kathy's dad, but he didn't know if she would spend the night with him or not.

Chapter 6

Christmas dinner with the Sturdivant family was interesting. Grant surprised everybody by bringing Sunny. They were all pleasant, but all having their own thoughts about why he brought her.

He broke off their engagement a few months before because she continuously lied to him. Sunny was convinced he was still in love with his deceased fiancée. He insisted on marriage counseling. That went sideways too. But he missed her and loved her and he went back; not knowing what the future held, not even what the next step was.

Chapter 7

For the first ten seconds Jacksa and Anderson were together they simply looked at each other. She touched his face with both hands, wanting to make sure he was real. The last time they saw each other it was via an app on the phone. Rubbing his face, she felt the beard he'd grown during the time he was away. It was cut close and shaped immaculately. He leaned toward her. Their lips touched, and they kissed; long, hard and passionately.

A few minutes later, they pulled into a garage. The driver opened the door, on Anderson's side of the vehicle. He got out, then reached back in with his "good" arm and took her hand. Neither of them said anything. The driver opened a door for them. In the dimly lit hall was an elevator. They held hands. The elevator door opened into a small living room. There was a balcony to the left and a small kitchen to the right. The door straight ahead was closed, but it was the bedroom. Jacksa started to cry. Anderson just held her. "Baby, I missed you so much. I was miserable without you. I am so, so sorry I couldn't call you, couldn't let you know I was alive."

"They told me you were presumed dead," she said between whimpers. She wiped her face with the back of her hands, and sat on the edge of the sofa. Anderson sat down beside her. He pulled her into his arms. The arm in the sling was across her back. She felt the weight of the cast. "Babe, what happened to your arm?"

He hesitated. "It's a long story."

Jacksa frowned.

"I promise to tell you tomorrow. For tonight I just want to hold you."

Suddenly there was a knock at the door, three taps. It startled Jacksa. Anderson kissed her hand, and got up from the sofa. He looked at his watch. It was midnight. He went to the door and tapped it three times. The look on Jacksa's face told Anderson she was afraid. "It's okay baby." He walked back over to where she was sitting. "It's just my security detail changing shifts. It's okay." He smiled at her. The fact there was a need for security made her very uneasy. "Come here." Jacksa went to him and they kissed again. He opened the bedroom door, they went in.

The light was low, but she could see the king sized bed, and flowers on the night stand. The bathroom was on the right.

"The closet is through the bathroom. There's stuff in there for you to put on." He pointed to the closet.

When Jacksa went in, it was obvious he had been there for a while. It looked like him.

Jacksa was in somewhat of a daze. She had so many questions that needed answers. She showered and changed quickly, went back into the bedroom, and crawled in bed beside Anderson.

"Thank you for the flowers."

"You're welcome. I know you want to talk, and we will, but not tonight."

"Nobody knows where I am, and you need to at least call Honey," Jacksa said to him seriously.
"Tomorrow. I promise," Anderson said.

She laid her head on his chest, and could hear his heart beating. They were both quiet. After a few minutes he started to caress her body. They made love for the first time.

Chapter 8

Hampton realized April hadn't come back from answering the door. He walked toward the door with Bryce in his arms. When he saw Lane standing there with April he knew something wasn't right.

"Bree, will you take the baby please?" Brianna took Bryce out of her grandfather's arms.

"Go back to the living room. I'll be right back," he said to her.

"April," Hampton called to her as he approached the foyer. She didn't look back. Lane did, and his expression spoke volumes. He stepped aside so Hampton could see their guest.

"Melissa, what the hell are you doing here?"

"Hello Hampton," she said with a smile. "Merry Christmas." Hampton didn't respond. "I see you have guests. I just wanted to see my daughter for my last Christmas."

Lane noticed that Melissa was holding on to the wall, and considering how long they stood there, she probably needed to sit.

"Hamp she's weak, and needs to go or come in and sit down," Lane said.

"Then she should go," April responded, and walked away from the door and back into the living room with the rest of the family.

"Good-bye Melissa," Hampton said waiting on her to walk away.

"Do you need help getting back to the car?" Lane asked.

Melissa sighed heavily. She looked up to see Hampton staring at her, but only held his gaze for a moment. "Yes please. Thank you."

    Lane took Melissa by the arm and walked her back to the waiting limousine. As they approached the car, the driver and a woman got out. They helped her into the back seat, and Lane went back to the house. He didn't know what April would say about him helping Melissa, but being a doctor made these types of situations his responsibility. He took his oath very seriously. He would make her understand. He needed a drink.

    Back in the house April had Bryce and Bradley in her lap feeding them sweet potatoes. If he hadn't known better, from the look of things you wouldn't know she just saw her mother after over twenty years. There was no evidence. Lane stopped at the bar, fixed a drink and joined Hampton and Ben in front of the television. They were watching the second game of the NBA triple header. The Spurs already beat the Bulls, the Cavaliers and Warriors were playing now. Celtics and Knicks still to come. Hampton didn't ask about Melissa and Lane didn't volunteer any information.

By half time of the third game everybody was asleep. April lightly kissed Lane on the forehead to awaken him. He looked up, smiled, and winked at her. They were only going upstairs to her apartment portion of the home she and her dad shared. April helped Belinda get the boys packed up. It took about 30 minutes to clear all the people out of the house. "Daddy I'll clean up tomorrow," April said to Hampton.

"Don't worry about it. We'll figure it out!" Hampton looked around and laughed.

Lane reached for April's hand, and headed toward the door. Hampton called her back.

"April, we need to talk about Melissa."

"Not tonight." She walked out the door.

Chapter 9

The sun caught her eye, as she came to full consciousness. For a moment Jacksa didn't recall where she was. Realizing she was naked she remembered. Glancing at the clock, she realized Anderson wasn't there. She panicked. The bedroom door was open. Her heart was pounding. The only sound was the hum of the refrigerator. Looking at the foot of the bed, she retrieved the gown she wore to bed. Slipping it over her head, Jacksa walked out of the bedroom, into the living room, and could see the ocean through the balcony doors. There were people in the water even at seven A.M., and others jogging on the beach. They were living their normal lives, and she didn't know what normal was anymore. With that thought she turned and faced the door, wondering if the security detail was still there.

Opening the refrigerator confirmed Anderson had been there for a while. His favorite beer was there, orange juice and cranberry juice which he liked to mix together and drink, and a gallon of milk, his other favorite drink. She poured orange juice into a glass and sat on the sofa holding the glass with trembling hands. She didn't know what to do or how to feel. Jacksa didn't know where Anderson was and didn't know if she should be concerned. Sipping the juice, she remembered the night before. How she felt to be in his arms; safe and secure. Waiting until they were married was the plan, but they had lost so much time, they didn't even talk about it. All they wanted in those moments was to be together.

"Do you trust me?" He had asked.

"Yes."

"Do you love me?" He asked.

"Yes, I love you."

"I love you too." Those were the only words uttered for what seemed like hours. They allowed their bodies to do the talking.

She finished the juice, sat the glass in the sink and decided to see what else was in the closet she could wear, and then shower. There were several things, all new, tags still on them. While standing there she got a whiff of Anderson's cologne. She walked closer to his clothes and inhaled deeply. She almost cried, thinking how she thought he was gone forever. But he wasn't. Her beloved Anderson was alive and Jacksa was so grateful.

Jacksa showered, and put on one of his t-shirts. Walking through the bedroom she heard the elevator and exhaled. He stepped off the elevator, and she saw the limo driver briefly before the door closed.

"Morning beautiful!"

"Good morning."

He kissed her cheek and walked past her. He had on workout gear and was sweaty and stinky.

"I expected you to still be in bed," he said from the bathroom.

"How do you work out with your arm in a cast?" Jacksa asked.

"You just don't work that arm," he said laughing. Before she could respond, he asked for some juice.

When he came from the bathroom, he was wearing only gym shorts. He looked amazing. Being half African American, and half Native American, he tanned easily, and it was obvious he spent some time in the sun. Jacksa's half African American, and half Asian American skin looked pale next to his, although she tanned more easily than most of her Asian friends. There were three knocks at the door. Anderson laughed.

"His ass is late as usual." Instead of tapping on the door in response, he opened it. The man on the other side was wearing workout clothes, and carrying a box. Anderson took the box from him, introduced him to Jacksa, thanked him, and he left. As he turned to leave she saw his "side arm" as Anderson called it.

"Let's eat," he said sitting the box on the table, and unpacking it. She couldn't believe he was acting so "normal" like he hadn't been out of touch with her for months.

The food smelled great and she realized how hungry she was. As they ate, he started to talk.
"Cutter was my partner during the operation, and requested to be my handler while I'm down here. He's a big country boy from South Carolina too, that's how we connected; except he pulls for the Gamecocks and I pull for the Tigers. That's where we draw the line."
Jacksa laughed.

"When we left Charlotte going to Memphis, Cutter's informant told him the plan had changed, and business was going to be handled in Biloxi. Cutter went to Biloxi and I went to Memphis, just in case. One of the suspects double crossed his people and I got stuck in the middle of the fray." He went on to tell her what he could about the situation. Jacksa asked a few questions, but she knew he wouldn't divulge but so much.

"Why did they tell me you were missing and presumed dead?"

"That was my CO's idea to throw off the suspects; in case they had people looking for me. I told him it wouldn't work. I knew you and Honey wouldn't go for it."

"So they knew you were FBI?" She asked.

"Yeah, my identity was compromised…" his voice trailed off. He wasn't sure how much to say for her sake. "His thought process was if my family, namely you, declared me legally dead, had a memorial service, it would be over."

"So I messed it up!"

"No baby, absolutely not. It went exactly like I told him it would."

"How did you break your arm?"

"Cutter and I got in a fight when he found me. This is the result." What Anderson didn't tell Jacksa, he had been beat up – bad. The arm was just the last thing to heal. He had some internal injuries, and was in the hospital for a couple of weeks. He also didn't tell her he shot and killed one of the suspects.

"How did you end up here, and why couldn't I know you were … alive?" She whispered the word "alive".

"I asked to come here. The bureau put me on mandatory medical leave, so I pressed the point!" He laughed.

"Mandatory medical leave for a broken arm? Anderson, you're not telling me the whole truth." Jacksa said very seriously.

He wasn't, and he couldn't. He looked at her seriously. "I had a concussion."

"Which means you hit your head."

"I was in a fight baby. I fell." He kept talking so she couldn't keep asking questions. "I couldn't tell you where I was until the bureau cleared me to."

"I hear you, and I understand that from your side, but can you put yourself in my shoes for a minute? I was devastated. I cried until I made myself sick. Honey, your mom and sisters were shattered. So were my parents. Honey was physically ill. Your mom was afraid she would have to put her in the hospital." Jacksa was crying, and Anderson had tears in his eyes.

Finally, he said quietly, "baby I was literally fighting for my life. I never intended to hurt you or my family." The tears were rolling down his face. He leaned forward, resting his elbows on his thighs, and covered his face with both hands. After a few seconds he leaned up, and looked at Jacksa. He cleared his throat. "This is what I signed up for. I knew the risk when I took the job. We talked about this Jack."

"We never talked about me thinking you were dead. We talked about undercover assignments, and long hours. We talked about the possibility of you getting hurt, but nothing like this. Nothing that almost caused your Grandmother to have a heart attack! No Anderson Thorn, we did not talk about that!"

They went back and forth for a few minutes, and finally he realized they were going around in circles. He said all he could say. He couldn't divulge any more information, for her safety. But he agreed to let his family know he was okay, starting with his grandmother.

"I will call her, break the news, and then you can talk to her," Jacksa said.

"Okay," was all he said.
"Which phone should I use?"

He handed her the phone the bureau gave her.

"I hope Honey answers. She doesn't know this number. No answer. Voice mail. "Hi Honey, it's Jacksa. Call me back on this number please."

They just looked at each other. Jacksa got up, and started clearing away the food containers. "If she doesn't call back in a few minutes, we need to call your mother," Jacksa said over her shoulder.

Chapter 10

Sterling texted Katherine quickly, and only said "ok."

He didn't know what they were doing, and he didn't want to deal with Katherine right then. He was glad she was on his side, but he had to call the shots, not her. He parked illegally, waiting to see Kathy walk out of the terminal. Shortly she emerged, pulling a bag behind her. Sterling jumped out of his SUV, kissed her quickly, and took the bag. He opened the door for her just as the security guard approached, and asked that he move his vehicle.

"Hey doll. How are you?" Sterling said as he pulled away from the curb.

"I'm good. Glad to see you!" She genuinely was.

"Will you spend the night with me? Your parents don't know you're in town."

She smiled slightly. "Yes, of course."

He reached over and touched her chin lightly. "You hungry?"

The thought of food made her feel sick. But she needed something.

"Yes, but can we go to the house and cook? I've wanted sweet potato fries and salad since you told me that yesterday!"

He laughed. "I got you baby!"

She willed herself not to change the expression on her face when he said, "baby."

They talked about football and her classes as they drove. When he turned off the exit to his house he pulled into the gas station convenience store. Kathy laughed. He looked at her, and made himself not laugh. "Would you like some chicken?"

"From the gas station?" She said continuing to laugh. "No, I'll pass."

"Okay, don't ask for a bite when we get to the house!"

Sterling sprinkled sea salt, and a cinnamon and brown sugar mixture on the fries, and put them in the oven. Kathy made the salad. He drank a beer, she drank water. She watched him move around the kitchen, and paid close attention to how he engaged her, and patted her on the bottom. He kissed her cheek, and forehead. "I wonder if things will always be this way," she thought to herself. She had to decide; tell him tonight or wait until tomorrow. He would be excited, but telling her parents wouldn't be as easy.

They ate, cleaned the kitchen, and basically went to separate corners to do work. Kathy was still in awe of how natural this all felt. She finished first, and laid on the sofa. Shortly after, Sterling asked if it would disturb her for him to watch game film on the television. "No, not at all, but I'm really tired. I think I'm going to bed."

"If you're getting in my bed, this will be a short film session!"

She rolled her eyes, he blew her a kiss.

A quick shower, and Kathy practically fell into bed. When she heard Sterling go in the bathroom, she had slept an hour. It seemed like minutes. She dozed off again, and awakened feeling Sterling's arms around her. She didn't bother to tell him there was no need to use the condom.

Chapter 11

"Sit down let's talk for a few minutes." Lane told April, and pointed to the love seat. There was something in the tone of his voice that kept her from arguing with him. "Are you pretending you're okay with your Mom?"

April didn't answer immediately. Lane waited.

"No, Lane, I really am okay. I don't care what she says or does. I am absolutely over her."

There was something in the tone of her voice that kept him from arguing with her. "Did you take a good look at her? She is not well," Lane said sincerely.

"Yes, I did. I saw the chapped lips, the dry skin, her clothes being too big. I don't miss much Lane. Just like I didn't miss you walking her back to her car."

"And..." again he waited.

"And, nothing. That's just who you are! I'm good with it. That's one of the things that attracted me to you." April was looking at him smiling. It was a seductive smile. Lane didn't know if that was her way of side stepping the conversation, but when she climbed in his lap and kissed him he didn't care.

Late that night, Lane awakened, and looked over at April. She was sleeping peacefully. He knew on many levels that April really didn't care. Her dying mother stood on the porch in the cold, and it did not phase April. Her actions made her appear cold, and indifferent, but "that isn't the April I know," he thought. This woman loved her father, her nieces, nephews, and even her sister, and it was out of character for her to be so unforgiving of her mother. As he thought about it, April didn't want to have anything to do with Belinda when she originally found out they were sisters. With that thought, Lane hoped she would make peace with Melissa like she did with Belinda. He also hoped it would be soon. From what he saw, time wasn't on their side. But, one thing Lane knew for sure, he had to let April make her own decisions.

Hampton sat on the sofa, looked around the room and laughed out loud. He was absolutely satisfied, delighted in fact, with the way the day went. His first Christmas dinner with his whole family. April and Belinda, his amazing daughters, who finally made peace. The truth – April made peace with him and Belinda. The icing on the cake, his four adorable grandchildren. He decided to take April up on her offer to clean up the next day. He kicked his shoes off, and laid back. The only hiccup of the day, Melissa showing up; unannounced, and uninvited. He appreciated that there was no scene, but he didn't appreciate her coming. He and April definitely needed to talk. From what he could see though, April was fine. She maintained her composure, and he was convinced she really didn't care about her mother. Melissa gave it a try. It didn't work. She needed to be okay with the effort, but move on. Like clockwork, the thought went through his mind, and the phone rang. It wasn't a number he had saved in his phone, but he recognized the New York area code. He knew it was Melissa or her assistant. He decided not to answer. Whatever it was, they could leave a message. If Melissa was dead, then his baby could really be rid of her mother. They didn't leave a message. Almost immediately, the message alert sounded. But it wasn't Melissa as he expected. It was Brittani.

"Thanks G-Pop for the best Christmas ever. Love you," and a heart emoji.

"Love you more," and two heart emojis was his reply.

Melissa knew calling Hampton was a long shot. She wasn't surprised he wouldn't answer. She was furious that April let her stand on the porch in the cold, and furious that Hampton didn't demand that April let her in. "He always did support her foolishness," Melissa thought.
"When she was 5 years old, and wanted to wear those rain boots with that velvet dress, and he told her it was okay…" Her thought trailed off. Truthfully, she didn't know how their relationship was. She wasn't there for most of it.

"But what difference does that make? I'm still her mother, and I won't be here next Christmas. Obviously he raised a brat."

Melissa was in denial. She didn't see anything wrong with leaving her daughter, and her husband to pursue her career, and being virtually absent for over twenty years. She also knew deep down April had every right to feel the way she felt.

Chapter 12

Jacksa's bureau issued phone rang an hour after leaving the message for Honey. She answered sounding as cheerful as she could. "Hi Honey!"

"Hello, how are you?"

"I'm good," Jacksa said, still standing, looking at Anderson.

"What are you doing today?"

Honey sighed. "I just came back from getting my hair washed, and I was going to work on the bumper guard and comforter for the baby bed I promised to make for a lady at church, but I don't feel like it."

Anderson motioned to Jacksa to move the conversation along. "Well, I need to tell you something." Honey sat, and held the phone tightly. "I got a call from the bureau…" Honey's heart was beating rapidly.… "they gave me an update on Anderson." Honey closed her eyes. Again Anderson made circular motions with his finger to make Jacksa move on. "He's alive Honey!"

"Anderson is alive." Honey said it very carefully. "Can you prove it Jacksa?"

"Yes ma'am…"

"So you talked to him?" I'm with him now." Silence. Anderson reached for the phone. Jacksa hesitated but gave it to him. Anderson took a deep breath.

"Hey Honey." There was a long moment of silence, and then he could hear her crying.

"Don't cry please," he said as tears swelled in his eyes.

"Where are you son?" Honey asked between sobs.

"I'm actually in Mexico."

Over the next few minutes Anderson and Honey talked, and he explained to her why he was in Mexico. He told her much less than he told Jacksa. When Honey was satisfied that he was fine, she asked if he wanted her to call his mother. "I will call her tomorrow. I promise."

When they hung up, Honey cried. She literally felt physically lighter. Her world was right side up again.

Anderson left the room for a few minutes. Jacksa just let him be. Next she needed to let her parents know where she was. She left the country, and didn't tell her parents or her brother.

Chapter 13

Sunny was walking on egg shells with Grant, and didn't like it. Christmas was fine, but he didn't give her the engagement ring back. He also hadn't mentioned marriage again.

She decided to push just a little, and see his reaction. "Babe, what are we doing for New Year's Eve?"

"I don't know, haven't even thought about it. What ya thinkin?" He asked.

She was glad for the opening. "I'm thinking we should go away; to New York or somewhere for a romantic weekend." Sunny was holding her breath.

"Don't wanna go to New York. Too much going on up there! Too many people. Check the flights to Vegas."

Sunny couldn't believe her ears. This was going better than she imagined. She went to the other room to get her tablet. They checked flights, and as it turned out nothing was reasonable. Sunny offered to pay for her own ticket. He said no, it was just too expensive this close to the day. Sunny was disappointed, but didn't react. "So what can we do?"

"Let's drive to Virginia Beach, get a spot with a fireplace, and watch the fireworks over the water." Grant looked at her, and smiled. She smiled back, but didn't really mean it. Virginia Beach, while quite nice, was a long way from New York City. She looked at him, and he was scrolling through some other site on her tablet. He was content with his plan.

Grant was good with the current status of his and Sunnys' relationship. He was staying at his place, and she was living in the townhome they once shared most nights. He loved Sunny but acknowledged he made too many missteps with her. Truthfully, he wasn't sure he could or should trust her.

He knew the suggestion of a romantic getaway was a seduction tactic. Grant didn't understand why Sunny thought she could sex her way to being his wife. Sex was never their problem. Their issues were outside the bedroom.

Grant's sister Gretchen was unhappy he reconciled with Sunny, and was verbal about it. The comment that rang especially loudly in Grant's ears was Gretchen's admonishment to him that Sunny may try to get pregnant. Grant didn't want to think Sunny would play that magnitude of game with him, but Gretchen convinced him she couldn't be trusted. Sunnys' romantic getaway would be punctuated with condoms.

The three-hour drive from D.C. to Virginia Beach was pleasant. Grant and Sunny talked, and laughed. No talk about their relationship, but about life; politics, sports, music, and movies. The weekend was off to a good start.

"We obviously weren't the only ones who decided to bring in the new year at the beach!" Sunny said, and they both laughed. There was a line of cars waiting in the hotel check-in line. When they were next in line, Sunny's phone rang. It was her mother calling from the Bahamas. "I got it, go ahead and talk," Grant told her.

"Good afternoon Sir. How may I serve you?" The desk clerk greeted Grant with a beautiful smile. He walked to the counter, totally mesmerized. He cleared his throat.

"Um, Grant, um Sturdivant checking in."

It is my pleasure to assist you Mr. Sturdivant. My name is Symphony." Her voice was soothing. Her smile was like light. Her eyes were sexy, her hair wild! She even had beautiful coffee with cream colored hands. He noticed her flawless manicure and no ring on her left hand when she gave him a form to complete. Her hand slightly brushed his when she gave him a pen. She chuckled. "Active military." Grant looked up. "Thank you for your service," Symphony said sincerely, looking directly into his eyes. Grant nodded and smiled. She noticed his dimples. He never knew what to say in these situations, and being so stunned by Symphony didn't help. "What branch?"

"Army," he answered, sliding the paper back to her.

"My dad is an Army vet, twenty-six years. I chose better!" She laughed.

Grant laughed too. "You active?" He asked.

"Retired two years ago. I was Air Force for ten years."

"Impressive," Grant said smiling at her.

"I'm in college full time at Norfolk State now."

"College full time and working. That's impressive too."

"Actually, this is my internship. My major is hospitality management." Symphony wanted to keep talking with Grant, but other people were waiting to check in.

"How many keys Mr. Sturdivant?"

"Um, two."

Symphony prepared the keys and handed them to him. "Enjoy your stay, and let me know if there's anything I can do to further assist you."

"Thank you Symphony, and thank you for your service."

She smiled.

Grant went back to the car to get their things, and to get Sunny. She was outside the car, and had taken out their bags. "Long line inside too?"

"Yep," was all he said. He gave her the key. "Go ahead to the room, it's cold out here," he pointed to the number, "and I'll be up as soon as I move the car. I'll get the bags."

"It's okay. I can roll them," she said smiling, and walked toward the doors.

Truthfully, Grant didn't want Symphony to see him with Sunny. As soon as he got in the car, Grant took a deep breath and blew it out loudly. He couldn't describe what just happened.

Chapter 14

Hampton's attorney's office called with the news. They had received a call from Melissa's attorney. She was in hospice care. The doctors stating it was a "matter of time."

"They are keeping her comfortable."

Hamp thanked them for the information. He sat for a few minutes deciding what to do. He decided to do nothing. There was no point in bothering April. If she really didn't care, the news wouldn't mean anything to her. If she was pretending she didn't care, that was one more act she would have to perform.

Lane added a splash of vodka to his orange juice, and then took the eggs out of the pan. Once on the plate, he added the hot sauce and laughed. April thought hot sauce on eggs was terrible. He missed her this morning. He had an early surgery, and she insisted he get sleep. The toast popped up, he grabbed it, and sat at the bar. A sip of vodka would be fine, he had two hours before he was due in surgery.

Surgery went well, and Lane wasn't on call, so he called April to tell her he would cook her dinner. "In other words, steak on the grill?" April asked and snickered.

"Oh! Is that a challenge Ms. Josephs?"

"Nope. A simple question."

"I can show you better than I can tell you!" He laughed.

"I'll bring the wine," April laughed too.

Lane knew not to mix his alcohol, but April showed up with Merlot and Riesling. The Merlot would work well with the Lasagna. April was impressed with the meal. Lane was a good cook, but most evenings when they could schedule dinner, they ate out. Their time was limited.

He finished his vodka on the rocks while he put the last touches on the salad, and waited for the bread to toast. Pouring April, a glass of wine, he placed her salad in front of her. The lasagna was setting. He finished his salad first, and served up the main course. They ate, they talked, they danced a bit, and went to bed. Lane went to sleep.

April got up early to leave. Lane didn't budge. She kissed his forehead, he opened his eyes.

"I'll talk to you later," she whispered, not wanting him to wake fully. He hugged her with his eyes closed. Walking through the kitchen to the garage, April noticed the wine bottle, and the vodka bottle on the counter. She thought a moment. Lane had at least two vodkas and two glasses of wine. She hadn't paid much attention at the time. They could talk about it later.

Chapter 15

"How soon do you have to go to campus?"

"Why? Are you trying to keep me in bed?"

Sterling looked at Kathy and smiled. Her heart was beating rapidly. She sat up in bed, and crossed her legs Indian style, and played with the bed sheet.

"What's wrong baby?" Sterling was sincerely concerned by her body language, and the tears in her eyes. "That crazy professor didn't contact you again did he?

She shook her head. "Sterling, I've been sick for a couple of weeks." Now he sat up. I went to the doctor yesterday…" Her voice cracked, then the tears came. Sterling pulled her into his arms. She sobbed heavily for a minute or two. Sterling's heart beat rapidly now too. He didn't know what she needed to say. He only hoped he would know how to respond. Finally, he held her by the shoulders, "what did the doctor say?"

"I'm pregnant Sterling. I'm having a baby."

For about ten seconds, neither of them said anything, and then the biggest smile ever came across his face. "Babe, that's great!" He hugged her. "Why you cryin'?"

"We're not married, I'm in school, all the other obvious reasons…"

He interrupted her. "What's obvious is that I love you. You love me, and that love created somebody else for us to love." He paused. She was looking down. He lifted her chin with his index finger. "Look at me." She met his eyes. "You havin' my baby is the best news of my life! Merry Christmas to me!" Sterling kissed Kathy, and then realized she was crying again.

"Babe, please! What is it?"

"Sterling, how can I tell my parents I'm pregnant and …"

He cut her off. "…and we're not married."

"Right."

"Kathy, this is not the sixties when people had shotgun weddings or the seventies when the expectation was marriage before children."

"I don't care what era it is, being pregnant and out of wedlock is wrong. It's out of order; out of God's order."

Sterling knew not to get in a debate with Kathy about God. "Hold that thought," he said, reaching for his phone. "What's up man? Pause. "It's all good. Not coming to campus today but call me if anything comes up." Pause. "No, I'm fine, have some family business to handle. "I'll see you at the party." Kathy just looked at Sterling.

"Come on. Get up, put some clothes on."

"Why, where are we going?" She asked.

"To get some breakfast." He got out of bed, took both her hands, and pulled her up. When she was on her feet, he put both arms around her, hugging her tightly. They lingered there, both quiet for at least a minute. He broke the embrace, patted her on the butt, and told her to go in the bathroom first. "I'll get you some water," he said. They both drank a bottle of water first thing in the morning. Walking downstairs to the kitchen, Sterling blew out a deep breath it seemed he had been holding since Kathy said the word "pregnant." His plan worked, and now he needed to execute part two; proposing to her. Grabbing the water, he was thinking as he went back upstairs. He heard the shower. That gave him a few minutes. He needed to move quickly, while she was still emotional. If he gave her time to think, she may reason something that would alter his plan.

Simultaneously the water stopped and her phone rang. He expected it was her mom. He reached for the phone, but didn't answer when he saw Michelle's name on the screen. He needed to talk to Katherine.

In the shower, Kathy thought about Sterling's reaction to her news. He was excited. The facts of the situation didn't seem to be important to him. "We are not ready for a baby. Neither of our lives is conducive to having a child. How in the world would we balance a child from New York to North Carolina? This is so complicated!" She sighed heavily.

Sterling came in the bathroom with the bottle of water. He smiled at her. She couldn't help but smile too. She drank almost half the water. He sat on the side of the tub, and sipped his water, and stared at her.

"What's the plan for today?" Kathy asked.

"I have a couple of errands to run, and at some point I need to deliver you to your parents," he laughed then continued, "since they don't know you in town! And…don't know you laid up all night wit yo man!"

Kathy rolled her eyes, and stifled a laugh.

During the ride, Kathy tried to engage Sterling in a conversation about their "situation." She was quite taken aback by his response. "First of all, don't call my kid a 'situation'. I know we have some things to work through, and we will, but not today. Can you please let me just have this for a day? You tellin' me we havin' a baby gave me life. I told you girl, all I ever wanted in this world is football and a family."

Chapter 16

The text message said, "Hi, it's Jacksa. Are you home? I need to call you from this phone."

Min frowned. "Jackson, come here please." Jackson walked into the bedroom, and Min gave him her phone. He read the text. "Do you think this is some kind of prank? She asked.

"No, she probably lost her phone or something. Go ahead and respond."

About two minutes later, Min's phone rang. "Hi Ma."

"Hi sweetie, who's number is this?"

Jacksa didn't answer the question. Is Daddy there? Can you put me on speaker?" Min pushed the speaker button.

"What's wrong Jacksa?"

"I am in Mexico."

"Mexico?" Min and Jackson said in unison.

"The bureau flew me down here…"

"Oh Lord. What is it honey? Do you know something about Anderson?" Min asked.

"Yes. He's alive. He's here. I'm with him."

The conversation with Jackson and Min proceeded much like the conversation with Honey.

Min cried, and Jackson was genuine in his comments. He was glad Anderson was alive, and safe.

After the call to her parents, Jacksa insisted they call Anderson's mother and sisters. Three times the tears, three times the questions, and a promise he would be home as soon as possible.

Phone calls made, they were both mentally exhausted. Anderson sat on the sofa and pulled Jacksa into his arms. With her head on his chest she listened to his heart beat. Neither of them said anything for a long while.

A knock at the door startled them. He looked at his watch and frowned. Taking Jacksa by the hand, he nodded toward the bedroom. Another knock. He mouthed, "close the door, be quiet." Her heart was pounding. He reached down and unstrapped a small hand gun from his ankle. She closed the bedroom door, but put her ear against it, trying to hear what was happening on the other side. Jacksa wished she had thought to grab a phone. There were voices but she couldn't make out what was being said. Then there were three voices, one with a Hispanic accent. Jacksa held her breath. Hearing the elevator, she became even more concerned. She turned the knob slowly, easing the door open. Only Anderson's voice, was detectable, but not clear enough to know what he was saying. Jacksa closed the door carefully, afraid to do anything else. Less than a minute later, everything was quiet, and Anderson was at the bedroom door. "It's okay Sugar."

She opened the door, and practically jumped into his arms. He explained it was another hotel guest, who was drunk, and at the wrong room. It sounded very simple the way he explained it, but Jacksa wasn't so sure. "Anderson, tell me the whole story. That was more than a drunk man not knowing where he was. How do you know it wasn't a set up? I saw you go for your weapon…that I didn't know you were carrying by the way."

"Yes you did, I told you on our first date, I am always armed."

"I didn't think that meant at home when we're alone."

Jacksa and Anderson went back and forth until they actually argued, both raising their voices. This was their first argument. Anderson was on defense because he thought the same thing. The drunk guy may have been sent by an enemy. If that was the case, the bureau would know soon, he was now in their custody. He couldn't tell Jacksa that. Maybe it was time for her to go home.

Chapter 17

The weekend at Virginia Beach was actually good. Sunny had a great time. Grant was attentive to her, and he let her call the shots. But the truth, he was distracted. He couldn't stop thinking about Symphony. He managed to avoid seeing her until time to check out. Symphony was at the desk alone.

"Good morning," she said pleasantly.

"Good morning."

"Checking out?"

"Yes." Grant was nervous.

"How was your stay?" Symphony asked smiling.

"Fine, thank you."

"Should I leave the charges on this card?"

"That's fine. Yes. Um, Symphony, may I call you?"

She was writing, and didn't look up. With the same beautiful smile, with which he was greeted, Symphony handed him a business card, a number was written on the back. He reached in his jacket pocket took out a card and gave it to her. His cell number was printed on his business card.

Back in D.C., Sunny expected Grant to move back in with her, but he didn't, he wouldn't. She screamed at him, and he left. The progress they made on the beach trip, down the drain. Back at his place, Grant called Gretchen, and his parents. After a few minutes on the phone with them, he turned his phone off.

After reading for a while, and then doing one hundred pushups, Grant turned his phone back on. Surprisingly there was no message from Sunny. On one hand he was glad. On the other hand, he was puzzled. This was out of character for her. Grant laughed, and said out loud, "I hope this isn't the quiet before the storm."

Symphony's card was laying on the dresser. Grant had picked it up, and put it down three or four times. Her card said "Symphony L. Sandhurst." He wondered what the "L" was for, and how she got a name like "Symphony". Her mobile number written on the card had a 318 area code. He looked it up, and discovered it was Shreveport, Louisiana. He knew there was an army base there, and wondered if her father was stationed there. Grant did something out of character for him, he went to his work computer and looked for the Sandhurst name to see if he could find anything on her father. The last name was uncommon so it shouldn't be hard to find. Or so he thought. There were thirteen people in the system with that last name, but not enough information to attach any of them to Symphony. Now he was even more intrigued. The mystery of Symphony Sandhurst could only be solved one way – asking her.

Sunny was the only person Grant had talked to or dated since Leah passed over four years ago. Their relationship naturally progressed because she worked in Human Resources at the hospital, and helped him get transferred, and settled back in the states. He hadn't just picked up the phone, and called a young lady since he met Leah in church all those years ago.

He was nervous, but he knew she wouldn't have given him her number if she wasn't available, interested, and wanted him to call. Grant took a deep breath, and dialed Symphony's number.

Symphony was studying. Along with her hospitality major, her minor was languages. She spoke fluent Spanish, French and German, and now was learning Japanese; the hardest of the four. The phone was on the other side of the room on purpose. Fortunately, there were no interruptions. She barely heard the ringing, and of course didn't recognize the number, and hesitated, but answered.

"Hi, this is Symphony."

"Good evening." Pause. "This is Grant Sturdivant."

"Hi Grant. How are you?" Symphony was smiling. Her voice was beautiful, and much softer than when she initially answered. It was soothing to Grant, and he felt guilty. He called her because Sunny was acting out. Just like he pursued a relationship with Sunny because he was grieving Leah.

"I'm good. How are you?"

"Physically fine, educationally challenged!" They both laughed.

"What ya workin' on?" Grant asked.

"I have to interpret an article from a magazine to Japanese, and I'm struggling. I should have stuck to what I know, but I had to add Japanese!"

As they talked she told him about her languages, and he shared he was previously stationed in Germany.

"I was in Germany too," Symphony said. "We lived there when I was in middle school for two years, and then I was stationed there for a year," she continued.

"I was stationed at Landstuhl Hospital there for four years. My specialty is Physical Therapy." They talked briefly about living in Germany. After a few minutes Grant realized he was keeping her from studying.

"What brought you back to the states?" Symphony asked.

"Can we pick up there in another conversation? I'm not allowing you to finish learning Japanese." He really didn't want to discuss the situation that brought him back to the states; Leah's illness, and his decision to stay after she died.

"Thanks for bustin' my bubble. I was doing just fine outside of reality!" She said sarcastically, and then laughed. Grant laughed too. "Well, okay," she said softly. "If you promise to call again."

He exhaled, hoping she didn't hear him. "I will call again," he said.

"Good night Mr. Sturdivant."

"Good night Ms. Sandhurst."

He let her disconnect the call. She went back to Japanese. He sat, and allowed his emotions to teeter; from curiosity to guilt, from guilt to not caring.

His phone rang as he sat, thinking about Symphony. It was Sunny. He didn't answer. She sent a text message. *"Going home in A.M. Emergency."* Grant looked at the clock. It was after eleven o'clock, but he cared about the emergency that was sending her home to the island of Eleuthera in the Bahamas. He called, pretended he had been asleep.

"My grandmother passed." He was genuinely sad to hear that news. They talked a few minutes, she gave him her travel details, and he offered to take her to the airport. She declined.

"I don't know when I'll be back."

"Okay," he replied.

Chapter 18

Sterling took Kathy to her parents' home, but didn't stay long, and made a point of not being alone with Katherine. He told Kathy he would pick her up for the party.

Feeling really good about himself, he drove to Charlotte, to the jewelry store. The jeweler he dealt with previously was waiting for him. He looked at both rings, and chose the marquise cut. He said it looked like a football. He put on a suit, put the ring in his inside jacket pocket, went to pick up Kathy, and on to the party.

Kathy was having an out of body experience. The room was completely silent. There was a faint scent of cinnamon. There was light above her head, but the perimeter was dim. Beneath her was a parquet floor, and Sterling was kneeling on that floor in front of her, and holding her hand. He was smiling, and looking up at her. She felt faint. His mouth was moving, but she couldn't hear him over the ringing in her ears. She closed her eyes for a few seconds. Opening them she felt tears roll down her cheeks, and heard him say; "Will you marry me?" Her answer had to be yes. She couldn't, wouldn't embarrass Sterling in front of his colleagues, and friends, nor embarrass her parents.

"Yes," she said, barely audible. He slid the ring onto her finger, stood and kissed her lightly on the lips, and then hugged her. The room erupted into cheers, and applause. Sterling looked up and caught Katherine's eye. She smiled, satisfied.

Kathy managed to make it through the rest of the evening. She smiled, accepted congratulations and showed off the ring to a whole lot of envious women. She didn't feel well. On top of the obvious emotions; the pregnancy and the surprise proposal, her stomach was queasy. There were too many smells. The mixture of food, and other holiday fragrances were making her sick.

Standing inside for a few minutes while Sterling got the car, was the first alone time Kathy had all night. She looked down at her hand. The ring was gorgeous. She knew her mother would be over the moon excited, and her dad wouldn't be happy about her being pregnant, but he would be satisfied they were getting married. Kathy's heart seemed to skip a beat. "Married? Married and ..." Before she could complete the thought, Sterling was walking toward her. She looked in his eyes. She loved him, but did not want to marry him.

Chapter 19

April had a challenging day, but was home now, and her two favorite people were coming for dinner; her dad and Lane. She picked up a meal from Hampton's favorite restaurant. He came upstairs before Lane arrived. Recapping his day, he told her about lunch with his identical twin granddaughters, Brittani and Briana. He was amused because they told him they had stopped dressing alike. April laughed as he recounted his visit with the twins. The food was warm, but April sat it in the oven warmer, so it would be nice and hot when Lane arrived.

When he hadn't arrived or called fifteen minutes after they expected him, April served Hamp's plate, and then her own. "Must be an emergency, it's unlike him not to call." They ate and talked, and finally April called Lane. No answer.

The phone startled him. He was lying across the bed, dressed, even wearing shoes. He looked at the clock, and realized he missed dinner. "Damn," he said aloud. The phone stopped ringing. He pulled himself up, and looked around for his glass. It was empty. He needed to call April back, but he couldn't sound like he just woke up. He cleared his throat, then went in the bathroom, and drank some water. Looking in the mirror he knew he couldn't go over there looking like that. He decided to call her from his hospital phone. He hardly ever used it.

"Hey babe, I was getting worried about you."

"Hey you. Forgive me. I had an emergency, and just finished.

"I told Daddy that's probably what happened. I called you a few minutes ago."

"My phone is downstairs in my locker," he lied.

"You coming over? I know you're hungry."

"I am. Let me tie up a couple loose ends and I will be on my way."

Lane felt awful; physically and for lying to April. He knew this story too well, and it didn't have a happy ending. He had to get himself together. He got in the shower, the water barely warm. Feeling better afterwards, he dressed in athletic gear, and drove to April's house. He needed her. He needed to feel her body next to his. He needed her to hold him close, and tightly.

 Hampton took advantage of his alone time with April. They hadn't talked about Melissa since the day after Christmas. That was almost a month ago.

"Your mom…ah…Melissa is in hospice." Hamp said it very casually, taking a bite of his bread.

"Yeah, I know," April said just as casually. "Her assistant sent me an email at work."

"Did you respond?" Hampton asked.

"Nope." She shrugged her shoulders.

"What do you plan to do when, and if she passes?"

"I don't plan to do anything Daddy. Why do you keep asking me that?" Her voice was even. She showed no emotion at all.

"You won't attend the memorial service?" He asked.

"Daddy please! Once and for all, no. I am not doing anything. A memorial service is a celebration of life. Why would I celebrate the life of someone I barely know? I know more about the cafeteria workers in our building than I know about Melissa Montgomery. If she leaves all that crap in place in her will, I intend to have it distributed just like I originally said; church paid off, the kids' education paid for, and that's it." She shrugged and changed the subject.

As Hampton and April discussed work, she heard the garage door. A couple of minutes later, Lane walked in. Kissing April on the forehead, shaking hands with Hampton, he then headed for the kitchen. April followed him, and offered to serve his plate. "I got it babe," he said. She patted him on the butt, and walked away. He looked over his shoulder at her and chuckled. She didn't know he wanted her hands on his butt, and he intended that to happen as soon as they could get rid of her dad. He wanted a drink, but he wouldn't do it. April was drinking water, and Hampton was drinking lemonade. He asked for water. He ate, they talked. He felt much better with food on his stomach. Just as Lane finished eating, Hamp left.

"How was your day?" Lane asked April.

"Fine until Daddy brought up Melissa being in Hospice."

"Did you tell him you already knew?" Lane asked, moving to stand behind her, and rub her shoulders.

"Yeah, and reiterated I don't care!"

He kissed her neck, and then put his arms around her. "April sweetheart, I had a hell of a day. I need your arms around me. I just need to feel you next to me."

There was something vulnerable about what Lane was saying, April thought. She wanted to ask what was wrong, but didn't. April took his hand, and lead him to the sofa. She sat and pulled him into her arms. They lay there quietly for a few minutes. She never thought of Lane as anything but strong, but right then he was not. He was cuddled up like a baby.

Without warning, Lane started to caress April, and kiss her, and then undress her. They made love on the sofa, and then just laid there for a while. When his phone rang he got up to answer, and she went to her room to get a robe. The call was about a patient. By the time he finished, the food was put away, and the kitchen straightened up.

He couldn't say no anymore. Lane fixed a drink. "Just one," he thought. He drank it slowly. It tasted good. He swished it around in his mouth. It felt good going down. When they went to bed, April fell asleep first. To keep from getting up to get a drink, he reached for her. She awakened easily, smiled, stretched and wrapped her legs around him. He rolled over on top of her. A few moments later, April shouted "Lane stop. You're hurting me!" He wasn't responding, and he didn't stop either. April bit his lip. When he lifted his head, she slapped him. "What the hell are you doing?" She screamed at him again. He snapped out of whatever was going on in his head. She pushed him off her.

Chapter 20

Sunny was gone two days before Grant reached out to her, and she hadn't communicated with him. It was early, but she answered. "Everything is fine. "The funeral is this morning," she said. She was hoarse, he knew from crying. Sunny told Grant her grandmother had a heart attack. "Granny was on medication for heart issues, but we, or at least I didn't know. My mom found out two weeks ago when the neighbor called saying Granny fell outside." Grant noticed Sunny's island accent. He was always amused how in such a short time with her family the accent came back.

"I'm really sorry you're having to deal with all this. Will you please tell your mother I extend my sympathy to her, to your family."

"Thank you Grant."

They didn't talk much longer. If an outsider heard the conversation, they would think these two people were merely friends, not two people who had a personal relationship, were lovers, lived together, and were once engaged.

Grant got ready for work, feeling sad for Sunny's family, but mostly glad for the break. He thought of Symphony. He started to call her, but decided to send her a text message instead.

"*Good morning. Have a phenomenal day. GS*"

She replied quickly. "*Good morning, Thank you. I hope the same for you. Talk later??*"

He replied. "*Absolutely.*"

Grant thought about Symphony all day. He was curious about her. When he was home that evening, he waited as long as he could before calling her.

"Hi Grant!" She sounded cheerful.

"Good evening how are you?"

"I am fine. I had an amazing day."

"Well let's hear all about it!" Grant said enthusiastically, and with a little chuckle.

Symphony went on to tell Grant that her manager submitted her name to the international Human Resources team to extend her internship. She was accepted, and will move to either Tokyo or Madrid in a few months.

"Nice! Congrats!"

"Thank you sir!"

He wasn't sure why, but the news of her moving away gave Grant a jolt. He had to say something. "So learning Japanese won't be in vain."

Symphony groaned in response. "Well yeah...there's that." They both laughed. She went on to tell him about the internship. He was quiet, trying to decide what to say and what not to say.

"Hello! Earth to Grant."

"Sorry, I was listening to you and thinking."

"Thinking what?" She asked.

"Thinking you will be leaving before we have a chance to get to know each other."

Symphony laughed.

"What's funny?" Grant asked.

"You. Sounding like you're really sincere."

"I am really sincere."

"Let's cut to the chase Grant. I'm attracted to you, you're attracted to me, but there's a problem."

He interrupted her. "What problem?"

She laughed again. "Playing dumb is not cute on you." He didn't respond.

"The lady in your life is the problem."

"How do you know…?"

She interrupted him before he could finish his sentence. "Grant, I don't miss much."

"Well it's complicated."

"Oh, my gosh! That is such a lame answer. It's not complicated. Either you're in a relationship with her or you're not. It's simple."

Grant was stunned. He and Symphony didn't know each other. This was their third conversation, yet she was challenging him.

"Symphony, my relationship with Sunny is complicated. That's not a cliché. There is a lot of back story."

"Is the back story a part of why you came back to the states?" Symphony's tone was softer. Grant inhaled and then exhaled loudly. There was a noticeable silence for a few seconds. With a slight chuckle, Grant finally said, "Sunny is a by-product of what brought me back to the states."

Over the next two hours Grant talked, and Symphony listened. She asked very few questions, and made even fewer comments. He told her about Leah, and how much he loved her. He shared in depth about her illness, and recovery, and her death. He talked candidly about his grieving process. Grant told Symphony how he decided to move to D.C. without Leah, because home wasn't "a good place" for him anymore. He even told her about Janis, including how she followed him after his and Leah's wedding party, and how they struggled over the gun.

"When I got to Walter Reed, I met Sunny. At first, she was the HR rep, then we became friends, and then we dated, and then we became lovers, and eventually I asked her to marry me."

"How much time passed between Leah's death, and you getting engaged to Sunny?" Symphony asked.

"Three years", he said and kept talking. It seemed cathartic for him to recount the events of his life, and Symphony was a good listener.

Grant continued by telling Symphony how Janis stalked him in Washington, and they both laughed when he told her about Sunny slapping Janis. His voice tapered off when he started to tell her about his relationship with Sunny falling apart. He ended that part of the conversation by telling her, "the trip to the beach for New Years was my attempt to get things back on track. We had a good weekend. But when we got home, she expected me to move back in, and for us to start making wedding plans again."

"Why did you…or should I say what made you get back together with her?" Symphony chose her words very carefully.

Before he answered Grant briefly thought about the night he went back, and that he took her home with him for Christmas.

"I missed her," He didn't say anymore.

Chapter 21

Lee and Katherine were waiting on Kathy and Sterling. As Kathy expected her mother was ecstatic they were engaged. Lee was a bit more reserved. He hugged Kathy, shook hands with Sterling and then made a joke about Sterling getting Kathy out of his pocket.

"After you pay for the wedding!" Katherine said.
"Give me a minute to get used to the idea Ma!" Kathy said, only half joking. About that time the door opened, and Kathy's cousin Michelle walked in singing.

Kathy and Michelle were also best friends, and Kathy was glad Michelle was there. She was the only person Kathy could trust. After about thirty minutes Kathy just couldn't take anymore. She wanted Sterling to go so she could lay down, and talk to Michelle. She made a comment about time to get out of the dress, and went to the kitchen. Catching Sterling's eye, he walked out of the room behind her. He put his hand on her shoulders, and kissed the back of her neck. "Let me help you out of that dress!" He whispered in her ear.

"You helping me out of my dress is why we're in this…" She was going to say "situation" but thought better of it based on Sterling's previous comment.

"Kathy, I didn't ask you to marry me because of the baby. I proposed to you because I love you, and want to spend the rest of my life with you." Her heart melted. "My original plan was New Year's Eve, I just moved up the timetable."

She smiled. "I need to lay down," she said. "I feel a little sick. Too many smells!"

He laughed, said okay, and took her hand. He kissed her lips. "I'll see you tomorrow." They walked back into the den, hand in hand.

Sterling left, Katherine and Lee went to their room, and Michelle and Kathy went upstairs. Kathy to her old room, and Michelle to the guest room. They changed, and Kathy laid on the bed, her head at the foot, and her feet propped up on the headboard. That position was the signal they needed to talk, as it had been since they were in high school. Michelle came in, and without saying anything she laid beside Kathy. Neither of them said anything for five minutes or so. Kathy's eyes were closed.

"I don't want to get married," she finally said.

"Why?" Michelle asked.

"I want to pursue my career."

"Why did you accept his proposal?"

" 'Cause I'm pregnant."

"That's not a reason to get married." Michelle didn't miss a beat. She was surprised, but not shocked.

"In my world it is." Kathy said.

"You mean in Aunt Kat and Uncle Lee's world."

"Yep!" Kathy said opening her eyes, and telling Michelle about the events leading up to the proposal.

"But you love Sterling."

"I do love him, but I don't want to be married, and I don't want children."

Michelle sat up, and looked at Kathy. "You're not thinking about having an abortion are you?"

"No, nothing like that. This is just not what I want for my life." Kathy said. "I want a Ph.D., behind my name, not an MRS in front of my name, a tenure track professorship, and eventually President, not wife and mom!"

"Don't you believe you can have all of that?" Michelle asked.

"I don't believe I can do it all well, and do it all in a reasonable time period."

"Reasonable is relative Kathy. Plus, you're not your Mom. You don't have to have an ultra-immaculate home, and flawless hair and makeup every time you leave the house. There's no requirement to chaperone every PTA field trip, and chair every PTA fundraiser. Do what you do, not what you saw Aunt Kat do!"

Kathy laid there thinking how easy Michelle made it sound. "The other part of the prob...," Kathy changed her wording, "the other part of the scenario is I live in New York and Sterling lives here in DavisTown. How is that going to work?"

"I don't know, but you have to give it a chance."

"Do I have to have a wedding?" Kathy asked seriously.

"No. Not if you don't want to, and yes Aunt Kat will get over it."

Chapter 22

Anderson and Cutter devised a plan A and a plan B. Plan A involved Jacksa, but they had to know if she could handle it, and was willing to. If the answer was no, or if Anderson sensed any hesitation on her part, he was sending her home. He loved her being there with him, but he needed to close this chapter in his life; professionally and personally.

Cutter wanted to present the plan to her. He insisted. "I'm not emotionally involved with her, so I can be matter-of-fact, and however she responds, I will be objective. Meet me at Luda's for dinner at 1800 hours, and you're buying."

"Damn man," was Anderson's reply.

Jacksa was glad they were going out. They spent most of their time in the suite, occasionally going to the beach. "Is Cutter married?" She asked Anderson as they were getting dressed."

"Yep, her name is Gia. We'll talk about that when we get back!" Anderson said laughing.

"What does that mean?"

"Nothing! I like her. I just want to see what you think."

Jacksa knew immediately upon meeting Gia why Anderson said they would talk about it when they got back. Physically they were the proverbial odd couple. Cutter was six feet two or three inches tall, and a very muscular two hundred pounds. Gia was tall too for a woman about five feet ten, and a lean one hundred thirty pounds. Cutter was white, bald, chewed tobacco, wore jeans and cowboy boots. Gia was black, with long locks, huge earrings, a dozen bracelets, a diamond stud in her nose, a long flowing dress, and very high heels. She had a Ph.D. in Fine Arts, and taught drama and creative writing at the University level. Gia was vegetarian, and Cutter's favorite food was a medium rare steak. She was going back to the states at the end of the week, in time to start the spring semester.

Jacksa liked Gia immediately. Even before Anderson introduced them, Gia leaned in for a peck on each of Jacksa's cheeks, and then did the same thing to him. At the table, Gia ordered in Spanish. "Your dialect is obviously not learned," Jacksa remarked. "No it's not. I was born in the U.S., but my mother is from the Dominican Republic. I lived there until I was thirteen. Gia went on to tell Jacksa and Anderson about her mother leaving the Dominican Republic and purposely coming to Florida so she would be born in the United States, "and so were four of my five cousins," she said. For the two hours they spent in the restaurant, Jacksa forgot about the current situation, and didn't even notice Anderson's security detail disbursed throughout the room.

Leaving the restaurant, Gia slipped off her shoes, locked her arms in Anderson's and headed toward the beach. Cutter put his arm out for Jacksa to balance and take off her shoes. Gia and Anderson were about ten yards in front of them.

"My wife the flirt," Cutter said, and they both laughed. "When are you and A.T. gettin' married?"

"I don't know," Jacksa sighed. "I guess when this drama is over."

Cutter got his opening more easily than he expected. "Do you want to help me end the drama?"

Jacksa slowed her stroll. She looked at Cutter frowning. "What can I do?"

"I have a plan, but you have to be all in. If you don't want to do it, say no, and I'm good with that. But if you say yes, there's no backing out. If you walk away mid-operation, it could compromise everything." They were standing still. Jacksa was looking down, and unconsciously digging her big toe into the sand. Cutter looked down the beach to see how far away Gia and Anderson were. She finally spoke up.

"Does Anderson know you're asking me to get involved?"

"Yep," Cutter answered very matter-of-factly. He noticed Gia and Anderson walking back towards them.

"Can he and I talk before I give you an answer?"

"Naw, that's too much emotion. You have to make a practical decision." The tone of Cutter's voice was stern.

Jacksa took a deep breath. "What if I can't…"

"You can," he said.

Chapter 23

April sat on the side of the bed looking at Lane. He had apologized for the way he acted, but April wasn't satisfied. His aggressive behavior puzzled her, and honestly frightened her.

"April, baby, I was a little drunk. I didn't mean to hurt you."

"Let's talk about you being 'a little drunk'." April said seriously. "You've been drinking a lot."

Lane could feel his face flush. He had been here before with his ex-wife; except she was screaming. April was speaking calmly. He had to play this off. "I haven't been drinking a lot."

"The last time you cooked for me you had at least two vodkas, and at least two glasses of wine."

"Damn!" He thought. "I had one vodka and the wine. I poured the vodka into the same glass I was already drinking from. And come on April, wine?" He laughed trying to minimize the seriousness of the conversation. April didn't say anything for a few minutes. Lane needed her to say something.

Finally, she said, "Lane you need to go."

"April. Please."

"I will call you tomorrow," she said, and walked into the other room.

Lane just stood there for a few minutes. When he realized she wasn't coming back, he got dressed. Walking into the great room, Lane saw April looking out the window. He paused for a moment.

April didn't look back. He took a few steps closer, but she didn't move. He put both arms around her, but no response. He kissed the back of her neck, and walked out. April turned out the lights and went to bed.

On the drive to his house, Lane replayed the evening in his mind. The circumstances were almost identical to what happened with his ex-wife. He needed a drink. He looked at the clock, never expecting to be headed home this time of morning. This was April's fault. If she let him stay he would be asleep now, and not walking into the house headed for the bar. He had one shot and went to bed.

Lane and April didn't communicate for two days. He wasn't sure what to do. They were scheduled to go to Houston for his former roommates wedding in three days. Lane told him he would confirm, by today, not knowing what would happen with Melissa, and not knowing if April would change her mind about attending the service. He decided to go by her office. She may ask him to leave, but they wouldn't argue. He also hadn't had a drink in two days.

April wasn't surprised when the receptionist told her Lane was there. She walked to the lobby with her cell phone in hand. "Hi," she said, and smiled.

He felt better. "Hey you!"

They walked back to her office. Lane looked at the sofa, looked at her, smiled and shrugged. The last time he was there, they made love on that sofa. April smiled too.

"I'm glad you're here, and I know we need to talk about some personal things, but I have something to tell you first."

"Sure babe. What's up?"

"Melissa died. I just got the call." She pointed to her phone.

She was not emotional, so Lane wouldn't ask her how she felt. "Did you change your mind about going to the service?"

"No," April answered.

He wanted to keep the conversation moving, but before he could say anything, the door opened, Hampton knocking and walking in at the same time.

"Oh, hey Lane." They shook hands. "Have you heard from …"

"Yes, I talked to the lawyer, and no I haven't changed my mind."

"There's nothing I can say…" Hampton was asking.

April interrupted him. "No, nothing, and Lane and I are going to Houston for a few days to his friend's wedding."

Lane was glad to hear her say that. For all he knew, she wasn't going, and decided to go now to hush the talk about her going to Melissa's service. He still wanted to talk to her; to let her know he wouldn't ever hurt her again.

Hampton didn't linger. April put him on the spot by asking if he was going to New York. "No," he said.

"Well, why do you think I should go? You knew her longer and better than I did."

"True, but she wasn't my mother."

April chuckled. "Mine either."

Alone again, Lane took advantage of the momentum. "I checked my schedule, we can leave Thursday if you want to," he said.

"Friday morning is still better for me."

"Okay, I'll confirm everything."

"You didn't come all the way over here to ask me that," April said.

"Yep, I did. I wanted to see you, and I didn't know if you would take my call."

April smiled slightly. "I love you Lane. We just need to work through that situation. We both had a couple days to think…"

"I love you too, and again I'm sorry. I won't ever hurt you again." Lane was serious. He decided not to tell her he wasn't drinking. That would make her think he was admitting there was a problem.

"Can you get outta here?" Lane asked.

"No, I have some work to finish, but I will meet you for dinner." "I'm done for the day, I can cook." There was hope in Lane's voice.

"I'm in the mood for pizza. How about I pick it up when I leave here, and we can eat at your house. You pick up the beer so it will be good and cold."

"Gotcha!" Lane smiled. He stood to leave, and pulled April in his arms. He kissed her forehead, looked at her and then glanced back at the sofa. She rolled her eyes at him.

Chapter 24

Lee and Katherine left for their annual holiday getaway, and Kathy was glad. Her mother was smothering her. She and Sterling needed to make some decisions, and make some plans.

Kathy got her thoughts together, and called Sterling. He convinced her to just bring her things and stay with him for the days she had left before going back to New York. Kathy was determined to have a plan before leaving town, and if being at his place would help precipitate that end, she was agreeable. Kathy knew she had to ease Sterling into the conversation. He was in denial about the complexity of their lives.

Sterling cut both of them a slice of sweet potato pie, and gave Kathy a glass of milk. He had coffee.

"Calcium not caffeine for my boy!" Sterling said sitting on the sofa beside her.

"So you think the baby is a boy?"

"I'm sure of it," Sterling said. "When do you see the doctor again."

"In a month. She will give me a due date, and make sure everything is fine. From my calculations, the baby should come in late July, early August." Kathy's tone was even.

"I'll get you moved back here in May as soon as school is out. I am going to hate not seeing you every day, but I want you to finish this year, so when you transfer you won't have any challenges." Sterling's voice was even too.

Kathy swallowed hard. She was stuck on the word "transfer", but she didn't want to argue.

"Sterling, I really want to get married now. I don't want a wedding, and I don't want to be pregnant and single."

"Well you should have thought about that before you seduced me!" He laughed. Kathy rolled her eyes. "I know you're serious. I know you want some conclusions." He paused for a moment. "Kathy I love you and I love our baby. I'm trying to think through all the pieces of this puzzle."

"So you admit this is complicated," she said.

"No, it's not complicated. We can get married Sunday, if we get the license today. Now I'm fine with that, but you know your Mom is going to be unhappy. At the end of the semester you move back here, and have our baby, and start our new life. I'll come up there as much as I can. When the baby goes to pre-school, then you can go back to school and finish your degree," Sterling said with satisfaction in his voice.

"You really have given this a lot of thought." Kathy said somewhat sarcastically. "And it didn't take you long to come up with a plan." She paused. Sterling didn't respond. "It's almost like you had this planned before I got pregnant." She paused again. He still didn't say anything. "The problem with your plan Sterling is it works for you, but not for me." He shifted in his seat. "I'm okay with the part about getting married Sunday, and you're right my mom will just have to get over me not having a wedding, but your plan goes all wrong after that. I'm not transferring at the end of the semester. I intend to graduate from NYU. And even if I would come back here to have the baby, there's no way I am waiting four years to go back to school." She laughed. "You cannot be serious to think I would even consider that!"

Sterling was looking at her, but he was actually surprised at her tone. He wasn't unfamiliar with it, just not expecting it. He thought the baby would take the edge off. He needed to get on offense quickly.

"Kathy we have to have money. I have to keep my job. I can't move to New York, and I'm not going to be away from my baby."

Kathy knew he meant that, but she couldn't give in and give up her dream. "I never wanted..." Kathy thought better of what she was about to say. She didn't want to hurt Sterling's feelings. "...you to be away from the baby, but I also didn't plan to be pregnant and still in school. The timing of all this is just a little off."

"God's timing is perfect Kathy."

"Then we have to believe God will work this out. I know He didn't give me the opportunity to be in school for just one semester."

"You know I'm not living apart from my wife."

"Sterling!"

"No compromise on that Kathy."

"Why do I have to make all the sacrifices...all the concessions?"

"That's not what I'm asking. You don't have to work, you can go to school and care for our family."

Kathy covered her face with both hands. She wanted to cry. What Sterling was offering, her cousin Michelle, and some of her friends wanted, but not her. They sat in silence for a few moments. "Sterling, I love you, and I'm getting used to the idea of having a baby, but you know I'm not the stay at home mom type. I want my career above all else."

Sterling looked at her hard. "Above all else," he repeated.

"Like you want football and a family, I want to educate young minds," she said.

There was a long silence between them this time. "Then I guess the solution is simple. We won't get married. You go back to New York next week. Come back here in May when the semester ends, have the baby and leave him with me. Then you can go back to New York and have your 'above all else'.

Chapter 25

Sunny was gone two weeks. She and Grant talked once or twice after the day of the funeral. When she called and asked him to pick her up at the airport, he couldn't refuse her. They didn't embrace, but he did take her bags and open the car door for her. Sunny told him about her time in Eleuthera, and seeing cousins she hadn't seen in years, and about her grandmother's service. Grant just listened.

They stopped for dinner, and then he took her home. Carrying her bags in, he looked around. It was her home, but they once shared it, and it was so cozy. He always felt welcomed there. "A place for everything and everything in its place," she said often citing that was her grandmother's rule. He hadn't been here in months, but it felt like home.

Grant rolled her bag into the bedroom, and again memories flooded his mind. He had to remind himself why he left. Sunny wanted presentation more than she wanted substance. Sunny walked into the room, brushing against Grant. Her contact with him brought him out of his daydream.

Walking back into the living room, he sat on the sofa trying to decide if he should stay long enough to make sure she was okay, or leave right away. Sunny walked in. "Thanks for picking me up."

"You're welcome."

"It was a long two weeks," she said sitting beside him, and taking his hand. He let her. Eventually Sunny apologized about the way things were when she left.

"Sunny we don't need to revisit that now."

"Just hear me out."

Before she could continue he told her he needed to leave. "Grant please don't leave. Spend the night. I just need some company."

"We've been here before…"

"I'm not trying to seduce you. I just want you to hold me until I go to sleep."

Grant knew he needed to stick to his guns, but he didn't. After a few minutes they went to bed.

    Sunny wore a teddy. Grant was in his boxers. She laid her head on his chest, and snuggled close. He put his arms around her. They dozed off. Shortly after, Grant's text alert on his phone sounded. He didn't budge, but Sunny eased out of his arms to look at the phone. Only the first few words of the message showed. She touched the screen to see the rest, but needed to enter the password. Sunny typed in Grant's birthdate, but that wasn't it. The second alert sounded to indicate the text hadn't been opened. He stirred a bit. Sunny sat very still. Holding the phone carefully, and placing the home button under Grant's thumb, she pressed gently, the screen changed, showing the apps including the text message app. New texts popped up. Sunny read one from Grant's trainer, a percent off coupon from the smoothie shop, and the most recent one; a message from someone named Symphony. It was casual but personal. She swiped the screen to scroll to the bottom, and read all the texts. The tone of them all was the same; casual, flirty and getting to know each other.

Sunny was furious! The more she read the angrier she became. Looking at the dates, she realized they met during her and Grant's New Year's celebration. Grant's texts to Symphony really outraged Sunny. He was obviously the initiator. The text message Symphony was responding to was Grant saying he was looking forward to seeing Symphony. Sunny shrieked, which awakened Grant. He sat up startled, and looked at her frowning.

"Who the hell is Symphony?" Sunny asked.

Grant didn't immediately realize Sunny was holding his phone. "Answer me Grant!"

"Sunny, what are you talking about?"

"Don't play with me. Who is Symphony?" She shook the phone in his face.

He had his bearings now, and snatched the phone from her hand. "Why do you have my phone?" Grant said getting out of bed, and getting his pants off the chair.

"You're not leaving until you explain to me who she is, and what your relationship is with her."

Grant put his shirt on before responding. "Why did you go through my phone?" He didn't raise his voice. He looked directly at her, waiting for an answer.

"I looked at your phone because I know you are cutting out on me." She was talking louder than necessary.

Still not raising his voice, Grant said to Sunny, "I am not cutting out on you, because we were done before you left for Eleuthera." She started to say something, but he kept talking. "When we came back from the beach you expected things to just pick up where we left off…"

"Yes, the beach. You met Symphony at the beach."

He didn't respond directly to that comment. "The trip to the beach was counterproductive. As soon as we got back you flipped the script. Sunny you are in need of something I can't give you. I want peace in my life. I want to love and be loved. You want to be loved and dictate to me how to do it. I have forgiven you over and over, I have started over with you more times that I should have. I knew tonight I should drop you off, and keep going, but I let you talk me into staying. Now you're invading my privacy." He had his shoes on, his keys in his hand, and walked into the living room to get his jacket. Sunny was right on his heels. "You're not leaving until I get an explanation," she said angrily.

"You just got an explanation. I'm done. You are not good for me." He stopped at the door, and looked back. Sunny stood there with a blank expression on her face.
"Good-bye Sunny."

The cold air hit Grant in the face as soon as he stepped outside, but it was actually refreshing. He felt good. Driving back to his apartment he didn't turn on the heat in the car. There was something freeing about the cold. He also turned off the radio. The quiet was peaceful.

In his apartment, in his own space, Grant laid on the sofa, and read Symphony's text message. It was late, and he wondered if she was still awake. He took a chance and responded. No answer so he knew she was asleep. "I will call her in the morning, and ask if I can visit this weekend," he thought.

Chapter 26

Bad weather in Atlanta delayed their flight, but they were fine. Lane was determined not to drink, and April was determined not to think about the conversation with her dad. He wanted her to reconsider, go to New York, and attend Melissa's memorial service. He even offered to go with her.

By the time they landed in Houston, got the rental car, and drove to the hotel, it was late afternoon. The rehearsal dinner was at 7:30, but they were both hungry. Deciding to order room service, April unpacked their things, and then turned on the television. Lane was on a call with another doctor, so she had the volume very low. The scene of a fire caught her eye, and then the picture switched to the anchor desk in a news room. The two reporters discussed the situation with the two alarm fire. As April watched and listened, the news anchors names appeared at the bottom of the screen. The female was "Tamara Silver." Her name caught April's attention. She knew Lane's ex-wife was a reporter. That had to be her! April watched more focused now to get a good look at her, when the report was back in the studio. The male anchor came back on screen said more at 6:00 and they went to commercial. When Lane was off the phone, April asked him if Tamara Silver was his ex-wife.

"Yep," was all he said.

When the news cast came on at 6:00, April was back in front of the television. She was very curious about the former Mrs. Lane Silver. This time she got a good look at her.

"Very attractive, cute dress and very flattering haircut."

"Did you know Tamara is still using your last name?" April asked Lane.

"Yeah, she established her career, in that name," he said.

"You okay with that?"

He shrugged. "I don't really care." He changed the subject. "Get your clothes on, traffic is bad in the direction we're going."

April knew Lane didn't want to talk about Tamara so she let it go.

He was like a kid in a toy store. Lane was glad to see his friends, and proud to show off April. He watched her work the room, smiling and laughing. His friends let him know how much they liked her. One friend saying; "Man, you know you boxing above your weight." At the end of dinner there was a champagne toast. Lane had one glass.

The wedding was a lovely affair, and the food at the reception was delicious. As everybody danced, mingled, ate cake and drank champagne, Lane and April wandered in separate directions. Standing in the cake line, April saw a familiar face, but couldn't call the lady's name, or remember where she knew her from. April decided to introduce herself. "Hi, I'm April Josephs."

"Nice to meet you April. I'm Tamara Silver."

April recovered quickly. "That's it. You're the news anchor. You looked familiar, but I couldn't place you."

Tamara laughed. "Happens all the time."

"I'm from the Atlanta area, and saw you on the news for the first time yesterday."

"Do you know the bride or the groom?" Tamara asked pleasantly.

"Indirectly the groom. I'm here with Lane."

"Oh, I see," Tamara wasn't smiling.

"Is something wrong Tamara?" April asked seriously.

"No. It just never crossed my mind that Lane would come."

"Is that a problem?" April asked frowning.
"Not a problem at all. Just haven't seen Lane in years, only once since we broke up and that was in divorce court. I heard he's doing well, and he's not drinking anymore."

April nodded toward an empty bench. Tamara hesitated, but took the few steps and sat beside April, who didn't vacillate.

"Why did you and Lane break up?"

Tamara considered her answer. "For several reasons. I didn't want children, he did." Lane had told April that. "I wanted to pursue my career, he wanted me to minimize it for the sake of a family." Lane gave April a version of that too. And I couldn't take the drinking." Lane had not disclosed that part of the story.
"Drinking?" April pretended to be puzzled. "That's the second time you mentioned that."

Tamara sighed heavily, waited a long moment, and took a bite of her cake; all before saying anything. "April, Lane and I were together a long time ago. Your situation with him I'm sure is very different. I think you should ask him."

"How do I ask him that out of the blue?" April asked.

Tamara gave some consideration to what April said. "Good point, but I don't want to prejudice you one way or the other."

"I'm not easily persuaded," April said.

"We met our freshman year at U of H. He was no different from the other guys; he went to class and partied on the weekends. He drank, but so did all the guys we hung out with. We broke up for a while when he was in med school, but when we got back together, he had stopped drinking. Over the years it was a roller coaster. He would get aggressive with me, apologize, stop drinking, but eventually start again. We went through that for a few of our married years. The night I told him I had no intention of getting pregnant, we had a big blow out. He got drunk and missed a surgery the next morning. I packed my stuff and left." April listened intently to what Tamara was saying. "I knew if he would miss a surgery, he was over the edge." April did well maintaining a puzzled look as Tamara continued to talk. "I grew up with a drunk daddy, if I wanted a child I wouldn't want him or her to grow up like that."

April needed to say something. She had to protect Lane, his reputation, and their relationship.
"Tamara, I'm a little flabbergasted by what you're telling me. That hasn't been my experience with Lane at all. He's an amazing man!" April smiled for emphasis.

"I am sincerely glad for you. Lane is a great guy. He just had some challenges, and I didn't have the fortitude to deal with them." As she started to say something else, a man walked over smiling, Tamara stood and reached for his hand. "Do you want cake?" She asked him, as they walked away. Tamara didn't look back. Sitting for another few minutes, April looked across the room for Lane. He was dancing with both four-year-old flower girls, and had a huge smile on his face. That was not the man Tamara just described.

April walked across the room. He saw her coming, and thought, "she is so beautiful." Just as the song ended, the best man was on the microphone asking all single men to come to the middle of the floor for the groom to throw the garter. "Whatcha think?" Lane asked April.

She laughed. "Go for it!"

He kissed her quickly, and joined the group. As soon as the garter was thrown the call came for the single ladies to come forward for the bride to throw the bouquet. The newlyweds left the reception to a hail of bird seed. April and Lane left a few minutes later holding hands. Back at the hotel, they changed clothes, talked for a while, and then Lane suggested they go to a jazz club later. April hesitated, "club" made her think he would drink. "Babe, we've been with other people all day, can we just have some alone time. Can you show me around before it gets too dark?"

"Of course Princess." Lane thought April was feeling bad about not going to Melissa's service in New York. That was far from the truth. She just didn't want him tempted in the club environment.

They rode around Houston for a couple of hours. While they were riding, April debated with herself whether to tell Lane about the conversation with Tamara. She decided to wait until they were back home in Landridge. Back in the hotel Lane turned on music, and they danced. He held her tight. "Love you April."

"Love you too," she said, holding him tighter. April was thinking she hadn't seen Lane have but two glasses of champagne all weekend, one at the rehearsal dinner toast, and one at the reception toast. She was fine with that. When they went to bed, he held her in his arms all night.

Chapter 27

Jacksa was dressed in a conservative gray pantsuit, and a black cape with a fur collar. She walked into the car dealership looking more confident than she was. Cutter sent her back to Charlotte on the same flight as Gia. Jacksa was living with Gia in their home temporarily, and found out on the flight back that the Bureau communicated with her parents, and her friend Nina, who was still taking care of Jacksa's dog Pepper.

Still a little bit uneasy about all this, Jacksa went over the plan in her head for probably the one hundredth time. Jacksa asked for Andre. The bureau showed her a picture of him, but when he approached her, she realized he was not as tall as she expected, and was wearing a shirt that showed his body builder physique. He extended his hand, they shook firmly.

"Right this way Ms. Baye."

"Call me Jacksa please."

The information Cutter shared with Jacksa was sparse. They were dealing with a gang called the Vultures. They were a subset of a gun Cartel out of South America. Anderson and Cutter had been investigating how they were acquiring the guns, and figured out they were up to something else.

"Yes ma'am." Andre showed her to an office.

"Did you get the documents I sent you?" Jacksa asked.

"I did, and I think we're interested in buying the car. Of course I need to see it first."

"Yes, of course. I understand. How soon do you think we can complete the transaction?"

"I don't have a firm buyer yet, but I am willing to take it on consignment for thirty days."

This was going almost verbatim to the way Cutter told her it would go.

"Andre, I hope you can appreciate my situation. I need the money as quickly as I can get it."

"Certainly Jacksa. We may have some options if you're willing to adjust the price."

Jacksa laughed. "I've done my homework. I know what it's worth, and I know how much Anderson paid for it."

He didn't react.

She stood and looked at her watch for emphasis. "I trust I'll hear from you by close of business tomorrow." Jacksa draped the cape around her shoulders, put her purse in the bend of her elbow and walked out.

Her heart was beating rapidly, but she was still better than she expected to be. As Cutter instructed she did not get on the phone, and drove about a mile to meet "Wendy Wolf" at a café. "Be aware of your surroundings" he told her.

Walking into the café, Wendy waved and Jacksa walked over smiling. They hugged. "Sorry I'm late," Jacksa said reaching for the menu.

"No problem," Wendy said. "I appreciate you meeting me on such short notice."

"I'm trying to sell Anderson's Corvette. I was referred to a broker, but I'm not sure we're going to do business."

Wendy and Jacksa kept the charade going through lunch. They didn't know who was in the café; who was following Jacksa. The bureau, Cutter and Anderson wanted the opposition to believe Jacksa thought Anderson was dead. She teetered between sadness and anger. Wendy asked, "Are you sure you want to part with the car?"

"No, I'm not sure, but I don't need it. I can't afford to keep it, and it just hurts too much to look at it every day," Jacksa said.

As soon as Jacksa left, Andre made a call. "Boss, the lady was here. The Asian lady."

"So she really wants to sell Thorn's car?" The boss asked.

"Looks that way," Andre replied. "Told me I ain't offering enough."

"Don't bicker wit her too much. Give her what she want. We need that car. She obviously don't know what it's really worth. The headlights alone…" The boss laughed.

"I'm 'spose to call her by end of day tomorrow."

"Aight, call round 4:30, offer her witin five gran' of what she askin'. If the lady presses you give her what she wants."

"Got it boss," Andre said shaking his head. "We shoulda took the car when we killed that fool."

"But as long as he's dead that's what counts," the boss said. Andre added, "It's funny how money make a grievin' widow, not so grief stricken!" They both laughed.

"So the stuff is hidden in the headlights," said the FBI agent who was listening to the call.

Chapter 28

Lying in bed alone looking at the ceiling, Kathy could barely hear the television. They had a big fight. He ended up leaving, and when he wasn't back two hours later, she went to bed. When he did come in, he stayed in the living room. She was at a complete loss. They were miles apart on this situation, and a very young baby was caught in the middle. Ultimately they wanted the same thing; to have a healthy, happy baby, but neither of them was willing to compromise. The truth of the matter was Kathy knew her parents and Michelle would be on Sterling's side. She was in this alone, and if she was going to earn a PhD at NYU, she would have to make peace with being alone, being a single mother, and defying her parents, and for that matter Sterling.

Sterling lay on the sofa thinking about the conversation he just had with Katherine. He went to his office to cool off and decided to call her. Kathy's mom was elated to hear she was pregnant, but like Sterling, surprised at her reaction. Their plan fell short.

Katherine and Sterling wanted Kathy back home. They decided together pregnancy, would cause Kathy to give up on school in New York, and return to Hattiesville. When Sterling told Katherine he put a pin hole in the condom, she was impressed at his ingenuity, and awaited the results. They hadn't considered

Kathy would opt to stay in New York. Katherine expected her to be so enamored with the baby, school would be secondary. Sterling repeated to Katherine, Kathy's "above all else" comment which really floored her. "I can't come home, Lee will question me, but I will go to New York next week and talk some sense into her!" Katherine said.

"How do you expect to accomplish that without telling her you know?" Sterling asked Katherine.

"I don't know," Katherine sighed, "but don't worry I'll handle it."

When Sterling awakened the next morning, he was still on the sofa. He stretched and chuckled. "This couch ain't comfortable," he thought. He didn't intend to sleep there, he fell asleep. Walking down the hall quietly, he saw the bedroom door was slightly ajar. Peeping in, he saw how sound Kathy was sleeping. All was right with the world in that moment but only God knew what the next few hours would be like.

He went to the kitchen, looked in the refrigerator, and pantry to see what he could come up with to cook breakfast. Getting that started he went to the bedroom to get Kathy up. "Hey sleeping beauty," he said patting her on the leg. She stirred and opened her eyes.
"Good morning."

"Breakfast in ten minutes."

"Okay," she said, and sat on the side of the bed. They didn't make eye contact. Kathy went to the bathroom and emerged a few minutes later with a sour look on her face.

"What's up babe?"

"Morning sickness," she sat at the table and closed her eyes. "I don't want anything to eat," she said without opening them.

"You have to eat something," Sterling said firmly."

"Just some dry toast please."

Sterling toasted two slices of whole wheat bread and fixed Kathy a cup of peppermint tea. "Eat it all," he said as he sat it in front of her. Neither of them said anything while she ate the first few bites of the toast, and he ate the full plate of food in front of him. "May I have a bite of your grits?" She asked. Sterling smiled and scooped a fork full of grits. Kathy leaned toward him, and he fed it to her. Both slices of toast and two forks full of grits, and Sterling was satisfied.

He gave her a bottle of water, and asked. "When are you going to New York?"

"I haven't looked at the flight schedule."

"You need to tell your parents we aren't getting married," he said. She knew he meant it.

"I'll wait until we make our final decision."
"You made it Kathy."

She just sighed.

Sterling cleaned up the kitchen. Kathy drank a second cup of tea, and remained at the table quietly. When he finished he asked if she wanted to go anywhere. "I'm going to the gym on campus, then to my office. You can take the car if you want to."

"Thanks. I think I'll catch up with Michelle. She's going back to Norfolk tomorrow, and I want to see her before she leaves.

While Sterling was working out he thought about Kathy seeing Michelle. He knew Kathy would confide in her about what was going on. He also knew Michelle would be on his side. This may get worked out after all.

Kathy and Michelle met at Kathy's parents' home. Nobody was there. They could talk candidly. Kathy was ready to defend her position. She knew she would need to. When Michelle pulled in, Kathy wasn't out of the car, but Michelle was on the phone. They waved, and Kathy went in, and straight to the bathroom. Michelle walked in smiling broadly. "That must have been somebody special the way you were grinning!" Kathy said to Michelle.

"He wants to be special," Michelle responded and laughed.

Michelle went to the refrigerator, got two bottles of apple juice, and they went to the sun porch. Kathy told her about the argument with Sterling. "You're still wearing the ring so I guess it's worked out," Michelle said.

"No, it's not worked out at all. I will probably go back to New York tomorrow. I just need to tell Mama and Daddy we're not getting married."

"You also need to tell them about the baby." Michelle put emphasis on "baby."

The tears in Kathy's eyes rolled down. She held her head in both hands for a few moments.

"I just don't know what to do. My daddy is going to flip, and Ma is going to want me to stay in Hattiesville."

"Kat, what's so bad about that? You have a man in your life who loves you, wants to marry you, and take care of you and your child! Why do you think you can't have that and a career?"

"I don't think I can't have both. I don't want both!"

"Then why did you accept Sterling's proposal, and why don't you have an abortion?" Michelle was screaming at Kathy.

"You know I'm not going to do that!" Kathy screamed back.

"What are you going to do?" Michelle asked but Kathy didn't answer. "Why can't you postpone your Ph.D. for the sake of the baby?"

"Because I don't want to be anybody's mama."

"Are you saying you wouldn't have a family if Sterling asked you to marry him, say four years from now?"

"No, I'm not. If I was out of school, and my career was intact, I would probably feel differently."

"So you had sex, which makes babies, and now you don't want to be a mother. How much sense does that make?"

"We used condoms. I had no reason to expect to get pregnant."

"So you're telling me the condom broke?" Michelle laughed sarcastically. "Do you know how ridiculous that sounds?"

"That's what happened Michelle."

"That's what Sterling told you Kathy. I suspect he lied."

"He wouldn't lie about something like that. He's not that guy," Kathy said dismissing the thought.

"Just for the record Kathy, I disagree with your decision. I think you should get married now, come back in May, have the baby and then transfer to a school closer. But whatever you decide to do, I'll help you." Michelle left shortly after without waiting to hear Kathy's response.

Lying on the sofa at her parents' house for a while, Kathy went over her options, and came to the same conclusion. She didn't want to be a wife and mother.

"Hey Sterling. Are you ready to go home?"

"I can be by the time you get here. What do you want to do for dinner?"

"I'm not hungry."

"Kathy Robinson!" Sterling said with a chuckle. She laughed too.

"I'll decide by the time I see you." That was the only decision she was going to make by that time.

Chapter 29

Symphony made sure Grant had a nice oceanfront room with a sitting area. There was a deep discount, but she wanted him to pay something, so there wouldn't be any misconception, or for him to think she had any agenda.

On the drive to Virginia, Grant thought about Leah, and he thought about Sunny. He didn't know if he wanted more than friendship with Symphony, and he didn't know what she wanted. Right now he wanted peace.

Sunny had called and texted a dozen times, but he didn't respond. What Grant knew for sure, he was off the Sunny rollercoaster. He was grateful for living on base, because she couldn't get to him unannounced.

Arriving at the hotel, he checked in and went to his room. Symphony left a message she was in class and would call him when she was done. For about two hours he sat on the balcony and alternated between reading, listening to music and dozing. It was cool, but the sun felt good on his face. The ringing phone interrupted the silence. It was Symphony asking Grant to meet her in the lobby. It was too early for dinner, so he kept on his jogging pants and hoodie. Symphony greeted him with a big smile and a hug. This was the first time he had seen her in casual clothes. She wore leggings and a long sleeve Air Force t-shirt.

"Really! Air Force! And you expect me to hang out with you," Grant said to her laughing.

"This will make you look better!" Symphony responded pointing to her shirt and laughing too.

Walking out a side door, and under a row of trees, they walked onto the beach, just strolling and talking until the sun went down. It seemed to get cold immediately. They ran back to the hotel.

"Do you want to get something to eat?" Grant asked.

"Yes, there's a place down the beach that's really good."

"That works."

"Are you tough enough to walk?" She asked laughing.

"Oh! The Air Force got jokes!

"No offense Army! I'm jus' sayin'!"

On the walk to the café, Grant's phone rang it was Sunny. He didn't answer. The phone rang twice more. The ringing phone wasn't lost on Symphony. Finally, she asked if he needed to answer. He was honest.

"No, it's Sunny." He told her about the last time he saw Sunny.

"Thank you for telling me. What do you plan to do? How do you plan to handle it?" She asked.

"I don't plan to handle it. I'm done.

"Do you expect she will just retreat?"

"I don't expect anything. At this very moment, my expectation revolves around you, and this weekend." Symphony smiled.

Walking back to the hotel, they locked arms and walked quickly. They didn't talk much. What they did say was generic; weather related or something about the scenery. Back in the lobby, Grant didn't know what to expect. It wasn't late and they had no planned schedule for the next day. They got cookies from the counter cookie jar, and got on the elevator. In the suite, Symphony reached for the remote and turned to the basketball game.
"Yes! My girl!
Symphony laughed and shook her head. They sat in front of the television.

"Are you a sports fan?" He asked her.

"Huge sports fan", she said. "If it's a ball, I'll watch it!"

Grant turned his fist to her and she bumped it with her fist. "So I'm clear. You watch baseball, golf and soccer too? He asked.

"Affirmative!" She said.

When the game was over they had talked more than watched. They had touched each other a lot. Symphony stood, stretched slightly, and asked Grant what he wanted to do the next day. Plans made, they hugged, held each other for a long moment, and Symphony left. Grant didn't want her to drive home alone, it was almost midnight.

"My apartment is less than ten minutes away, right across the bridge, and I will call you when I get there."

Standing on the balcony Grant could hear the water, but he couldn't see it. This felt right. Being with Symphony felt right. "Symphony Lillian Sandhurst," Grant said aloud and smiled. She shared with him the "L" was for Lillian. "My paternal great grandmother, and my maternal grandmother were both Lillian. If I ever have a daughter, her name will be Lillian." He made up his mind in that moment he wanted to be Lillian's father.

Chapter 30

April decided to keep her conversations with Tamara to herself. Lane was great, not drinking, and being very accountable.

The office was in a frenzy, due to a deadline for a proposal to the City of Landridge. April's policy was all proposals were to be submitted three business days in advance. They had two days to meet her schedule. Hampton's executive assistant Felecia, knocked on April's door.

"Yes."

"April, Hampton needs to see you in his office," Felecia said. April looked up from her work, clearly annoyed. Before April could respond, Felecia said, "No it can't wait."

Rolling her eyes, April grabbed a note pad from her desk and walked past Felecia, who followed her to Hampton's office. The force with which she opened the door let him know she didn't want to be there. He was sitting at the conference table not at his desk.

"Yes sir!" April said, sitting across from him. Felecia sat in her regular seat, on his right. Hampton didn't address her attitude.

"I know you're busy, but this can't wait. I have the estate documents from Melissa's assistant. You need to sign them so she can wrap this up."

"You interrupted me for that?"

Felecia cut her eyes at Hampton.

"Why didn't you just sign my name on it? Damn!"

Hampton slid the papers across the table without responding to her comment. April took a deep breath, and removed the packet from the envelope. There was a page, and a half letter she didn't read. Page three was the distribution list. Taking another deep breath, she made sure the list showed the money for the church, the scholarships for her nieces and nephews and the other things previously indicated. Satisfied with what she saw, April signed, and slid the paper back across the table to her Dad, stood and walked out.

"She didn't read the letter," Felecia said to Hampton.

He shrugged, "I know," he sighed. Just send them a note of regret on her behalf. I don't know why Melissa thought April would sit on her foundation board."

In her office April fumed, glad that was over, but so tired of Hampton trying to act like this was normal. She slammed the television remote to the table. The batteries popped out. One hit the table, one hit the floor. She picked up the one on the floor and threw it against the hard hat on her credenza.

Reaching for her phone she called Lane, expecting to leave him a message. He answered.

"Hey doll! This is a pleasant surprise."

"Are you busy?"

He heard something in her voice he didn't like. "Doing some notes for a consult with another surgeon. Why? You want me to come over there, and put you on that sofa in your office?"

She managed to laugh. "Not quite, but can you meet me at your house?"

"Now?" Lane was glad April couldn't see the expression on his face.

Taking a deep breath, April calmed a tad, and told Lane, "I need a hug, a drink, some comfort food…"

He laughed slightly. "Okay sweetie, can you give me a couple hours?"

She didn't respond.

"Go to my house, I'll be there as quickly as I can. Call me when you get there, I'll undo the alarm."

"Thank you," she said sincerely, picking up her purse, walking through the break room, and out the back door.

When Lane got home, April was asleep in the recliner, wearing workout clothes. He leaned down and kissed her forehead. "Is that food I smell?" She climbed out of the recliner and followed him to the kitchen.

"Yes ma'am. One of your favorites." Lane pulled a container from the bag. April squealed like a little girl. He drove across town to one of their favorite restaurants, and bought her chicken mac and cheese. They sat at the island in the kitchen and ate it out of the "to go" container, and drank too sweet iced tea. When they were done, April headed back to the recliner. "No ya don't! Come on," Lane said extending his hand. Like a little girl she took his hand and followed him through the kitchen into the garage and got in the car. He knew something was wrong when she didn't reach for her phone. He drove downtown, parked, and April never asked where they were going. Also unusual for her. They walked a block, and Lane rented two bicycles. At this point April started laughing. They rode for over an hour through downtown, around the park, pass the church and through the Landridge historic district.

"Whew! I need a shower," April said putting the bicycle in the rack.

"I can help you with that!" Lane said, and grabbed her around the waist.

"I think I will let you," she said kissing his lips lightly.

A warm soapy shower, passionate love making, and one glass of wine each, they lay in bed together, not talking, April playing with Lane's fingers. He sat up, pulled her in his arms, her head on his shoulder.

"Tell me what set you off today," Lane said quietly.

She sat up, crossed her legs Indian style, took both Lane's hands in hers, and told him about the papers, and the phone call.

"When I was six years old my dad and I went on vacation for two weeks. When we got back all my things were at his house, and Melissa had gone to Paris. I did not see her again for over twenty years when she showed up last Christmas. There is nothing normal about that! So why all of a sudden does everybody think it is normal for me to go to her memorial service, or care what happens to her estate? Or to care what the hell even happened to her? Why do people think that's normal? Why does my dad think that's normal? And why in the world would she think I want to sit on the board of her foundation? I don't care she had cancer, I don't care that she's dead, and I don't care to sit on her board! Why would they even call and ask me that?"

Lane hadn't said anything. He kept his eyes on April, listening intently. He had to respond correctly. She kept talking.

"As far as I'm concerned, this whole situation is over now. She tried to manipulate me as a child. I'm not a child anymore. I am a grown ass woman with my own things. I don't need her, I don't need her money, I don't need her foundation. I don't need anything that has to do with Melissa. I gave away the money, and I don't want any more. Why won't her people, and my dad just leave me alone?"

Lane took both April's hands and kissed them. "Sweetheart, they are going to leave you alone. Consider that handled. You don't have to answer anymore inquiries from anybody; personal or professional. I believe you and support you. I got you babe."

He pulled her back in his arms. He held her thinking she was going to cry. She didn't. She was not shaking. She was not emotional. He knew in that moment, if he had ever questioned it, April was so very serious. She did not give a damn, and had moved on. Continuing to hold her, they both went to sleep.

Chapter 31

The Bureau issued phone rang. It was Andre. Jacksa took a deep breath and answered. The phone was recording the conversation.

"This is Andre. When can you come back so we can make a deal on the 'Vette?"

"I can't come back if you're going to waste my time. My price isn't going to change, and I have another interested buyer. We make a deal today, or I'm moving on." Jacksa sounded confident, and to an extent she was. She knew this was the only way to end this madness, and get Anderson home. There was still a lot about the operation she didn't know; for her safety Cutter told her. He also told her she was doing fine with the car fence.

In the midst of the original operation, the Corvette that was supposed to be Anderson's was in the possession of the dealers. When the fight and eventual shoot out occurred, the police recovered the car. The word got out through an informant that the car was returned to Anderson's family. The plan after a respectable period of time was to sell it. The bureau knew they would reach the top of the pyramid with the car being involved.

Jacksa successfully negotiated a deal with Andre for the car. They made arrangements for him to have it picked up the next morning at the facility where it was stored. "I need to be sure there isn't anything personal in the trunk. I forgot to check," she said quietly, with reflection, looking off into space. Andre briefly felt sad for her.

"I will have a certified check for you," he said and shook her hand.

Simultaneously special agents were installing tracking devices on the car. They accounted for an expectation of Andre's cohorts watching the car.

As instructed, Jacksa went back to Gia and Cutter's house. She was paranoid of being followed, and then remembered there were agents following her, so if the dealers had the audacity to make a move, the agents would intercept them. Jacksa just hoped nothing would go down.

In the house Gia called Cutter on the bureau issued landline phone, and put him on speaker. She was careful not to handle the phone.

"Good work Jacksa," Cutter said. "All you have to do now is show up in the morning, accept the check and give him the envelope from the glove compartment."

"What if it's not Andre?" She asked.
"Good question. Don't hand the envelope over to anyone

else. Demand to see Andre or tell them the deal is off. Don't worry we will have eyes and ears on you.

"Okay," Jacksa said barely audible.

"And Jacksa, Thorn is fine, and he loves you."

She started to cry. "I love him too," she said between sobs.

Chapter 32

Sterling was tired…mentally. His plan to get Kathy back home wasn't working and the reality was he needed to come up with an alternate plan. That plan could involve being a single parent, which was not doable for him. Katherine Robinson helped him devise this scheme, and she needed to help him get this together. The truth, he didn't take Kathy at her word early in their relationship when she told him she wanted a career more than a family.

Back at Sterling's house they cooked, ate, and cleaned the kitchen together. There wasn't any discussion about the future, but it was the elephant in the room.

The alarm sounded early the next morning. Kathy felt Sterling get out of bed, but she didn't awaken completely. A little later, he kissed her forehead. "I'll be back in a couple of hours. If you need me, call me.

"Okay, but I'll be fine."

When the door closed, Kathy exhaled loudly. It was a breath she held for twelve hours.

Lying on her back, Kathy practiced what she would say to Sterling, and her parents. First, she would give Sterling the ring back, thank him for wanting to be her husband, but saying she didn't want to be his wife; not anybody's wife. Next, tell her parents about the baby. Knowing there would be discussion, Kathy would just have to be prepared to defend herself.

Part three of the conversation would be the hardest. Kathy would say to all three of them that she planned to come back in May. The baby should be due in July. "Maybe it will come July fourth, then I can declare my independence," she said aloud. Six or seven weeks after, go back to New York, and leave the baby with Sterling.

None of what she intended to say to them was negotiable. Not even for her dad, who was her biggest fan, her toughest critic, and her harshest judge. Kathy dozed off again, satisfied with her plan.

While he was out, Sterling called Katherine. He took a chance she would answer. She was alone, and Sterling quickly brought her up to speed. "I will be home tomorrow, and invite you two for dinner. I will handle this," Katherine said confidently.

Back at the house, Kathy was making brownies when Sterling came in. He laughed. "Brownies at nine in the morning!" She laughed too.

"I had a taste for brownies and bacon."

"I didn't expect the cravings to start this soon," Sterling said. She paused for a moment, realizing it was actually a craving.

They were both relaxed, feeling good about their own plan. Later that day Sterling and Kathy ran errands, went to a movie, did a little shopping. It was an ordinary day.

"Hi Mama. Are you back?" Katherine was calling Kathy as promised. For a few minutes they talked about Lee and Katherine's trip. Sterling kept his eyes on the television, and his ears tuned to Kathy's conversation.

"Let me ask. I'll call you back. Sterling…"

"Yes, Babe."

"My mom wants us to come for dinner tomorrow."

"Okay." He pretended to be distracted by the football game on television.

"Sterling, can we talk a minute?"

He hit the mute button on the television, and looked at Kathy.

"I want to tell Mama and Daddy about the baby tomorrow since we're going to be there. She paused for effect. That definitely wasn't all she wanted to tell them.

"Are you prepared emotionally to have that conversation?" He asked, sounding very serious.

"I'm not sure, but it needs to be done," she responded. "You know I got your back baby."

Kathy smiled.

Chapter 33

The knock at the door had to be Symphony. Nobody else knew he was there. He opened without looking through the peep hole. He laughed immediately. She wore a navy blue Air Force sweatshirt and jogging pants, and Nike tennis shoes and hat. "Let's go Army. PT on the beach."

"I don't have anything to wear."

"I don't believe you for one second. Ya'll take that gray and black everywhere!"

He laughed. "I got you Air Force." He dressed and they ran down the steps rather than take the elevator. "Can we have some breakfast?" Grant asked.

With an absolute exasperated look on her face, she replied, "Protein and beverage only. I don't want any excuses out there."

Bacon, eggs, coffee and juice for Grant. Bacon, eggs, fruit and water for Symphony. While they were eating a man and woman came to their table, shook hands with them and he said, "Thank you for your service."

"Yes sir, they said in unison."

Once outside they stretched, and started running at a steady pace. At about fifty yards Grant broke into a sprint. Symphony kept up. At about one hundred yards, she pointed to an access area that lead to the street. They jogged pass a few businesses that were just opening. Pink, red and silver balloons caught Grant's eye. "Tomorrow is Valentine's Day", he thought to himself. "I have to figure out how to do something for Symphony without her knowing."

All of a sudden Symphony broke into a sprint, but Grant caught her. Ahead of them was a small park. They stopped running and walked to an obstacle course. Once through the course they walked back to the beach access holding hands.

"Much respect Air Force. Impressive work out."

Symphony smiled and took a bow. They jogged back to the hotel.

"Can I have some food now?" Grant asked.

"Sure," Symphony said.

Grant piled on the food this time. Waffles, bacon, eggs, oatmeal and hash browns. Symphony was amazed. "I have stuff to do this afternoon, but I want you to come over for dinner this evening."

"I would love to. Thanks. What should I bring?"

"Nothing. I have it all covered. I will text you the address."

When they finished eating, Grant walked Symphony to her car. He leaned in for a peck on the lips. She blushed.

Back in his room he googled some stores, showered, dressed, and went shopping.

Sunny called and texted.

Chapter 34

April woke up to breakfast in bed, a dozen long stem red roses, and a red velvet box on the tray beside her plate. Literally holding her breath, she opened the box. Inside was a pair of stunning diamond earrings. With a huge gasp, April said, "Lane these are…I can't think of a word…absolutely gorgeous. Thank you." She leaned in and kissed him.

"Happy Valentine's Day darling! You're welcome."

April was moving the box around so that the morning sun hit the diamonds at different angles. They sparkled, and threw a reflection on the wall. She was smiling and there was a light in her eyes only rivaled by the diamonds. "So I did good?" Lane asked smiling.

"You did good," she said with emphasis on "good."

"Well, if you like that you're going to love this." He reached under the bed, and pulled out a black velvet box, opened it to reveal a two carat diamond ring that exactly matched the earrings. On his knee he took the ring from the box, and took her hand. "I love you April. Will you marry me?"

Shocked and surprised, the proposal was unexpected. They talked in general about marriage, and a future together, but she wasn't expecting this. Lane was holding his breath now. Her pause lasted only a moment, but it seemed longer to him. "I love you too." Her voice was barely above a whisper. She paused again. His heart was pounding, He expected her to say no. Maybe what Tamara said got to her. "It will be my honor to be your wife." He slipped the ring on her finger. He got up from his knees, and pulled her into his arms. When they let go, and he looked at her, she was crying. "Why are you crying?"

"I am so happy. I never thought I would get married, but sometime I would wonder if it happened how I would be proposed to."

This was a different vibe for them. April was showing Lane a side of her he never saw. A softer more vulnerable side. She was always in control, usually in charge; calling the shots, running the show. Now she was exposed and sensitive. They were in unchartered waters. Lane liked this side of her.

April didn't know Lane talked to her dad, and got his blessing before he bought the ring. She also didn't know he talked to her sister Belinda about the ring. So when they sent pictures to Belinda and her twin daughters, Brittani and Brianna, only the girls were surprised.

When they went downstairs to see her dad, he opened a bottle of Dom Perignon for a toast. Later in the evening they went to dinner. At the restaurant Lane told April he was skeptical about the traditional Valentine's Day proposal.

"It was such a surprise; it doesn't matter what day! That was actually a good move because I would expect you not to propose on a traditional day, so flipping it around was genius!"

What Lane didn't tell April; he talked to Tamara. She had called him. After her conversation with April, Tamara felt uneasy. Maybe she said too much. What if Lane was really different, what if he had worked through his drinking issue?

Tamara was honest with Lane, telling him everything she said to April. Immediately he was furious, and told her so. "Why in the hell do you think having that conversation was the right thing to do?" Lane was loud, and he was angry.

"Lane, you don't need to raise your voice," Tamara said just to buy a few seconds. As she thought about it over the days Tamara wondered if maybe she was jealous things didn't work for them. Was she offended because April asked; because she dared to approach her, and wanted to discuss her ex-husband? "April came to me. Introduced herself, and started asking me questions."

"Did she ask you about my past problem with drinking?"

"Not directly."

"What does that mean?" Lane asked.

"She asked me why we broke up." Now Tamara was loud.

"Wow Tam! So you took it upon yourself to sabotage my relationship?" Before she could defend herself, he continued. "Because you didn't want a family, and never bothered to admit that, and lied about the pills, don't mess with me and April."

There was silence for a few seconds. Finally, Tamara said, "Lane I didn't call you to argue. I simply wanted you to know she asked why we broke up. I told her the truth including I refused to have a drunk for a husband!"

"You are a damn trip. Stay out of my life Tamara."

He bought the earrings and the ring the next day.

Chapter 35

When Andre arrived at the auto storage he didn't expect Jacksa to already be there. He wanted to wait on her, not have her wait on him. He was ten minutes early.

Jacksa's heart was beating so hard she could hear it. If this went wrong, there could be dire consequences. She and Cutter talked very early in the morning on Gia's phone. There was no change of plan, and he reassured Jacksa all would be fine.

Taking a deep breath, Jacksa slowly got out of her car. She looked sad, but in fact she was terrified. Andre greeted her warmly, and after the formal pleasantries were exchanged, he asked her to have a seat in his car to go over the papers. She declined stating, "I'm fine where I am. Taking the papers, and looking through them page by page, Jacksa actually found a mistake, and didn't know what she should do. There wasn't anybody to ask. Frowning, the only option was to take matters into her own hands. The mistake was probably a set up.

"Andre there seems to be a mistake here." She pointed to the error.

"Damnit," said Andre's people who were listening, "she caught it."

"Good eye," Cutter's person said, "But now what?"

"Give her a minute, she's doing fine."
"Why don't we just make the correction, both initial and finish this up?" Andre said.

Jacksa looked at him and smiled. "Do you know what I do for a living? Her question caught him off guard.

"No, why?" His tone was harsher than he intended it to be.

"I'm a paralegal. I look at contracts every day, and I know making a change like that on a document like this is illegal."

"Shit!" Andre's cohort said from the car they arrived in. He put his hand on his gun. If Andre gave the signal, he would use it, and force Miss Paralegal to sign. Simultaneously, Cutter's people were preparing for Andre to make the wrong move.

Chapter 36

The day was uneventful, and they were both pretty quiet while getting dressed for dinner with the Robinsons. Sterling was certain Kathy's parents would be able to convince her to marry him now, and come back to Hattiesville to stay at the end of the semester. They would have their baby and live the life he always envisioned. He was willing to make some concessions. Kathy wanted to be a college professor and president, he could get a job on the coaching staff at a larger college or university, maybe even the NFL. Although Sterling loved DavisTown College, and the Hattiesville/DavisTown community, he was willing to move.

"Man, I know we've talked about you flirting with my wife," Bishop Robinson said when he walked into the foyer and Sterling was presenting Katherine with the flowers he brought her. They all laughed. As Sterling hung up their jackets, Katherine and Kathy walked into the kitchen. Kathy asked her mother about their trip. Katherine raved about the hotel and the food.

"I bet the food can't compare to what you cooked Mrs. R.," Sterling said putting his arm around Katherine.
"He's at it again Daddy."
"I see him.

"... and that's why my faves are on the stove!" Sterling said laughing.

He was right. Katherine was saying thank you for making their plan work. Sterling piled his plate high with barbeque ribs, steamed cabbage, and baked sweet potatoes. He wanted to eat before Kathy sprang the news on her parents.

The dinner conversation was easy. By the time Katherine brought out the pound cake, Kathy's courage was up. She took Sterling's hand which made her mother smile. Katherine laid her head on Lee's shoulder. Kathy squeezed his hand, let it go, and then slipped the ring off her finger, laid it in his palm, and closed his hand around it. "Thank you for wanting to be my husband. I'm honored you chose me, but I don't want to be your wife. I don't want to be anybody's wife." Katherine sat up straight. Her mouth was open, but her voice wasn't working. Kathy kept talking. "Mama, Daddy, I'm pregnant. Sterling and I are going to have a baby." Her dad shifted uncomfortably in the chair, and folded his hands in front of him.

"You're having a baby, but calling off the engagement! How much sense does that make?" Katherine asked. Sterling had laid his fork down, and leaned against the back of the chair. He wasn't moving his head, he just moved his eyes from one person to the other. There was a lump in his throat the size of a golf ball. Kathy didn't respond directly to her mother's comment. "I'm leaving tomorrow. I will be back in March for spring break, and back in May for the summer. The baby should come in July. I will stay here six or seven weeks, and then I'm going back to New York…"

"My baby…"
"Sterling, the baby will stay here with you."

Sterling looked at Kathy with sheer fury in his eyes. Nobody was saying anything. Katherine looked at Sterling, but he wouldn't make eye contact with her.

"How did you arrive at this plan, and making all these decisions, obviously without counsel?" Lee was asking Kathy, looking directly at her. Kathy didn't answer immediately. "The look on Sterling's face attests to the fact he wasn't aware of your intentions," Lee continued.

"Sterling and I talked…" Kathy started saying.

Sterling interrupted her. "We talked about reaching a compromise, we never talked about you giving me back your ring." His voice cracked. He cleared his throat. "And we did not talk about you leaving the baby with me."

"I told you I want my career, not a family."

"Your exact words were you want a career 'above all else.'"

"Kathy Robinson! When did career become more important than family?" Katherine raised her voice. Lee patted his wife's hand.

"It's not Mama, and that's exactly why I never wanted a family." Kathy was very calm.

"Sterling is a reasonable man. How do you think he's feeling?" Lee Robinson was an unlikely ally, but Sterling was grateful. "I'm confident he will reach a consensus with you. He is doing the honorable thing. Do you want to be pregnant and unmarried? Do you want to have a child out of wedlock?"

"No Daddy, that's not what I want."

Lee looked from Sterling to Kathy, and back to Sterling.

"You all decided to have sex outside of marriage, and didn't do anything to prevent pregnancy, and now you want to shirk your responsibility." The tone of her dad's voice, and his body language hurt Kathy's feelings.

"Bishop, Kathy didn't make this baby by herself. I'm responsible too. But, I didn't ask Kathy to marry me just because she's pregnant. I admit that changed the timing, but I love Kathy. I want to spend the rest of my life with her. She is the woman I want to be the mother of my children.

As they talked Kathy got angry. The three of them acted like she wasn't in the room. They also failed to realize nothing any of them said was going to change her mind. Then it happened.

"Kathy, think about what happened to Leah. Your sister wanted children, and Leah didn't live to have any. How can you say you don't want to be a wife to Sterling, and a mother?" Her mother's voice was soft. Kathy laughed.

"So there it is. You finally said it!" They all looked puzzled. Sterling was pretending. He knew what she meant. Kathy continued. "This is not about me, or my baby. This is about Leah. If she was still living you wouldn't care if I had a baby or not."

"That's not true Kathy, and you know it," Lee said.

"I don't mean you wouldn't love this grandchild too, but it wouldn't matter if he or she was here or in New York. You know Ma…" Kathy's voice cracked, …Leah was the one who wanted the domestic life not me." Katherine didn't respond. Kathy looked at Sterling who looked hurt. Finally, he spoke.

"It's okay, Bishop, Mrs. R. Let Kathy have her freedom. Let her have her independence. I will not stand in her way. I ask two things. One, please take care of yourself so the baby is healthy. Two—be absolutely sure this is what you want. Because, if you go through with this plan of yours, and leave the baby with me, you will have to sign away your rights. I will not allow you to run in and out of my baby's life." His voice firm, tears in his eyes, and his face expressionless, but Kathy knew he meant every word he just uttered. Sterling did not waste words. A few moments of silence in the room, then he got up from the table. Sterling looked at Katherine, then Lee, and then Kathy. He half smiled. "You are the only woman I ever loved." With that he walked out.

Outside he let the few tears fall, wiped his eyes and started the car. Sterling's and for that matter Katherine's plan for Kathy to get pregnant had worked. Their anticipated response from her had not. He needed to come up with another plan; on his own this time.

Chapter 37

"My girl!" Cutter was laughing at Jacksa. For a few minutes Jacksa, Cutter, Gia and Anderson were on the phone. Jacksa was delighted to hear Anderson's voice. Cutter told Gia and Anderson about Jacksa "handling" Andre. After about five minutes Gia and Anderson disconnected from the call, and Cutter explained to Jacksa what their next move was.

After Jacksa exposed Andre's flaw in the contract, and refused to make the adjustment, she actually challenged him.

"Ms. Baye, I have a buyer for the car. I assured him I will deliver today."

"Andre, you shouldn't make promises you didn't know you could keep. Legally, until your check clears the bank it's not your car."

Andre cursed under his breath. "I will re-do the contract, and make the correction."

Jacksa was looking over the document again, and that annoyed Andre. She knew he was looking at her and waiting for an answer. She didn't look up until she glanced at the last page. Then Jacksa took the pen and drew a big circle around the section needing correction.

"I don't see anything else we need to edit," she said, handing the contract back to him. He looked at her with disdain.

"Can you meet me back here this afternoon?" Andre asked.

Jacksa looked at her watch. "No, but I can meet you here tomorrow morning, same time."

He had no choice but to accept, but he pressed one last time. "What do I tell my buyer?"

"You don't have a buyer. At the moment you don't have anything to sell!"

Jacksa explained to Cutter that the clause in the contract she zeroed in on was indeed in error. "I wasn't sure what to do, but my instinct said he did it intentionally."

"No doubt. This jackass knows just enough to be dangerous. He knows a flaw like that wouldn't make him liable in court."

They talked a few more minutes. Cutter told her to stick to the original plan when she met Andre the next morning.

Chapter 38

Grant didn't know Symphony well enough to make an educated guess about what she liked. She wore silver jewelry, the same perfume his sister wore, and purple was her favorite color. He didn't know the name of the perfume, but he would recognize the bottle. He knew he was safe with flowers, perfume, and jewelry.

Symphony stopped at the grocery store, bought everything she needed and headed home to tidy up her place. She texted Grant her address, and told him to be there at six o'clock.

Grant did his shopping, except for the flowers, and checked the directions to see how long it would take him to get from the hotel to her apartment. Twelve minutes according to the GPS.

The temperature had dropped noticeably. The wind blowing off the ocean was cold. Grant drove to the florist, picked up the large bouquet of lavender roses he ordered earlier that day. Fifteen minutes later, he arrived at

Symphony's apartment. When she opened the door, the roses were hiding his face. She laughed, and invited him in.

The aroma in the apartment was tantalizing. It literally made his mouth water. He looked around. The space was small, but cozy. The balcony overlooked a dimly lit pier, with about a dozen boats. Symphony sat the flowers on the coffee table. She hugged Grant and thanked him. They held each other for a long moment. Grant broke the embrace. "What did you cook? It smells good!"

"Wash your hands, and I'll show you!"

He came back to the table, covered with wax paper over newspaper. She motioned for him to sit, and brought over a pot, and dumped the contents on the wax paper. There were crab legs, corn, potatoes, sausage, crawfish, and shrimp. She gave him a beer, a bottle of water, and a roll of paper towels. Grant had a boyish light in his eyes. "Damn girl!" He said as he reached for a cluster of crab legs. Symphony slid the melted butter, kept warm with a small candle underneath, across the table. "I can't take you home, my daddy wouldn't let you leave. He loves seafood."

"Well, I'll just have to go to Hattiesville and cook for him."

When they finished eating, Grant was stuffed, and deliriously happy. "We need to go for a walk."

"It's cold," was Symphony's response.
"Ten minutes?"

"How about I put on some music and we dance," she countered.

They danced, and she sang. Her voice was amazing. After a while, he took her hand and walked to the love seat, the lone piece of real furniture in the room. There were two director's chairs, a coffee table, and a book shelf where the television sat. They all appeared to be flea market or thrift store finds.

"I brought you something. He gave her the wrapped box. She was excited!

"Thank you." she said opening the box of perfume. "I can't believe you figured this out!" She took the top off the bottle for a quick spray. But hanging around the neck of the bottle was something else.

Grant took the perfume bottle from her, and took the diamond ring off the bottle's neck. Holding her left hand in his right hand, he knelt and said "Symphony, will you marry me?"

As though it were the most natural thing in the world she said, "Yes."

There was no thought to the fact they had known each other a little over a month. This was the second time she'd seen him. What they knew about each other came from hours on the phone.

"I mean today, on Valentine's Day. Will you marry me today?" Grant waited.

"Yes, I will marry you today."

They shared their first real kiss. After a short discussion about not telling their families until after they were married, Symphony packed a bag, and went back to the hotel with Grant. On the ride over the bridge she said matter-of-factly, "I need a dress."

"We'll shop first thing in the morning. I need a suit."

They stayed up late talking about where they could get married, and living arrangements. Finally, Symphony asked the question; the one dealing with the elephant in the room. "What are you going to do about Sunny?"

"When I get back to D.C. I will let her know I am a married man."

Symphony smiled.

At some point during the night, Symphony decided she wanted to get married in D.C. rather than in Virginia.

"If that's what you want, I can call the Chaplin and I know he'll marry us. We will have to make it legal on Monday, but we'll be married."

"Yes, that's what I want to do."

When the mall opened at 10:00 they were there, deciding Symphony should get a dress, but he would wear his dress uniform. The bridal shop had the perfect white dress in her size. In about an hour, Grant and Symphony were on the road to D.C.

The hospital Chaplin agreed to marry them at 6:00 PM. They needed two witnesses.

"Do you know anybody in D.C. you want to call? Grant asked.

Symphony thought for a moment. "No I don't think so. My cousin is there, but I can't tell her not to tell her mother, who will tell my mother, and I want to do that myself."

Grant chuckled. "I have two co-workers I can call. They're a married couple."

"Okay, do it!"

"Now, she's going to ask a bunch of questions, and—she knows about Sunny."

"If that doesn't bother you, it doesn't bother me," Symphony said.

"I know what I'm doing. I'm confident in the fact I want to spend the rest of my life with you." Grant was serious. He looked over at Symphony who had a slight smile on her face.

"We do need to make one stop before we get into the city." Symphony said.

"Where? Why?" Grant asked.

"I need to buy you a ring." She reached over and held his hand, then looked at the diamond on her left hand. Symphony knew marrying someone she'd only known for six weeks was crazy, but somewhere in her heart it felt right.

At 5:40 P.M. when they arrived at the chapel, Grant's friends were already there waiting. He made the introductions, and Symphony thanked them for participating in the ceremony. Grant had squashed his friend's questions on the phone earlier, and asked her to just be there for him and Symphony and let the past, especially Sunny go. They brought Symphony a bouquet of purple flowers.

At exactly 5:55 P.M. they walked into the chapel, and at 6:00 the Chaplin began the short ceremony. They exchanged silver wedding bands, and posed for pictures. The Chaplin reminded them to get the license the next day for him to sign. The friends took them to dinner, they toasted with champagne, and celebrated their Valentine's Day marriage.

Chapter 39

Kathy, Sterling, Katherine nor Lee got a good night's sleep. All for different reasons. Lee was stunned at Kathy's actions; from being pregnant to saying she would give the baby to Sterling. Katherine was appalled. Nowhere in her thought process did she consider Kathy wouldn't move back to Hattiesville, get married, and have the baby. They would be a family in Hattiesville, not a family in two states. Katherine pondered Kathy's comment about Leah, quickly dismissing it. Katherine missed Leah tremendously, and wished she'd lived, married Grant and had children. But this situation was about Kathy not Leah. *"Kathy just needs to do the right thing,"* she thought.

Kathy didn't sleep because Sterling walked out. She didn't expect him to just accept what she said, but the look on his face was worse than expected. It was indescribable. He left her at her parents' house, and her things were at his. Kathy didn't know if Sterling intended to take her to the airport or not. She thought they would go back to his house, talk and create a plan; an arrangement that worked for both of them.

Sterling's emotions ran the spectrum. On the drive home, he remembered her things were at his house. As soon as he was home, he gathered what wasn't already packed, drove back across town, and left the bag on her parents' front porch. He went to the gym hoping the workout would relieve the stress, tire him out, and he would go to sleep. He lay there looking at the ceiling. None of that had worked. He hated to do it to Kathy, but he had one more play he could run; another woman. One thing he knew for sure, even when women say they don't want you, they still don't want anybody else to have you. By the time the sun came up, he knew what he had to do.

Chapter 40

Standing outside the car, Andre was waiting for Jacksa with the revised contract in hand. She pretended to talk on her phone, smiling broadly, and pretending to laugh, and made him wait.

"Forgive my delay," she finally said. "I need to tell you about that call. Are you familiar with Hendrick Cordoba?"

"The football player. Yes, why?"

"That was his agent. Cordoba wants to buy the car."

Andre's countenance changed. "Did you tell him you have a buyer?"

Jacksa chuckled. "Of course I did, but he is offering more for it; thousands more."

Jacksa was not telling the truth. Cutter wanted to make Andre uncomfortable, and see how much negotiating he was willing to do. If the Bureau totally misconstrued this, he would walk away. If he negotiated they were right; the car held the key to blowing open this operation.

"Ms. Baye, we have a deal. Cordoba can't show up now, and buy the car from under me."

"Andre, the contract is in your hands, unsigned. I can do whatever I want. I can sell the car to whoever I want to sell it to! It's my car!" Her voice cracked, truthfully from nervousness, but it sounded like sadness, like she was about to cry. Jacksa turned away from Andre momentarily and cleared her throat. Taking a deep breath, she told him; "The price just went up."

Andre and Jacksa debated for a few minutes, and he agreed to pay what she told him Cordoba was willing to pay. What wasn't lost on Cutter, Andre's agitation, and his willingness to meet Jacksa's price. She insisted he follow her to the bank to get a certified check for the updated amount. He countered saying he could have the client wire the difference to her account. That confirmed for Cutter there was no legitimate bank account. Agreeing to those terms, thirty minutes later, the transaction was complete. Jacksa and Andre shook hands. The tears in her eyes were genuine. She was relieved to be done with this, and to know she helped Anderson solve this crime so he could come home. The ball was in the Bureau's court. While she didn't know what would happen now, she knew the end to this situation wouldn't be as long as it had been.

Next, Jacksa was going back home. Back to her own house, and back to her job tomorrow. First, she would text her friend Nina. Hopefully she was home. Jacksa wanted to pick up her dog Pepper. He would bring some normalcy. "Tomorrow I will visit my parents," she said aloud.

Nina and Jacksa talked about half an hour. Jacksa told her what she could, and Nina shared that Wendy Wolfe had contacted her twice to assure her Jacksa was fine. "I am really glad you had a good vacation," Nina said as Jacksa was leaving, and "let's have brunch this weekend. I need to tell you about Wilson!" Nina rolled her eyes, and Jacksa laughed.

Chapter 41

Saturday was girl's day out. April took her nieces shopping, and Belinda met them for lunch. The girls enlisted their mother's help in convincing April to have a traditional wedding.

"Sorry girls. I agree with Aunt April," Belinda said.

Brittani and Briana looked at each other and frowned. "We'll execute plan B!" Briana said, picking up her menu.

April looked at Brittani, "What is plan B? And please don't say G-Pop."

Brittani only smiled. Briana changed the subject. They fully intended to talk to Lane.

April wanted to be a June bride with a beautiful white dress. She wanted her dad to give her away, and a man waiting at the altar in a white dinner jacket. But she didn't want hundreds of people, and bridesmaids with matching dresses and bouquets.

"Well then Auntie, what about a destination wedding?

"Why do you know so much about weddings?" April asked Briana.

"Research!"

The foursome laughed.

"A destination wedding is an option, but where?"

Before anybody answered the server brought their food. Once they were settled, Brittani answered. "How about the Hawaiian Islands?"

As the conversation continued, the options became Maui, and an intimate ceremony at their church.
"I'll talk it over with Lane, and let you know." April said looking at Briana.

"By the way, who's paying for the wedding?"

"Briana!" Belinda said, "That is not your business."

"I'm not being nosey. I just read that in a traditional marriage, the father of the bride pays."
Brittani chimed in, "But in destination weddings which are more contemporary, the bride and groom usually pay themselves."

Belinda and April looked at each other and shrugged.

"How was girls shopping day?" Lane asked April.

"Pretty intense actually."

Lane frowned, and looked at April seriously. "What happened?"

"My nieces are just too much."

April told Lane about the wedding discussion, and asked what he thought.

"I think I want to be your husband, and how we make that happen...." He shrugged.

"You don't care?"

"I care," he said, "But I'm just more interested in the end result."

"But if you had to vote…"

"If I had to vote….let me think about it."

Lane didn't want to say the wrong thing. He was glad the target date was only four months away. He was doing well, and he needed to stay on track. The stress of a wedding wasn't what he wanted or needed.

As he tuned back in to what April was saying, his phone rang. He laughed and showed April the screen. It was Briana.

For fifteen minutes the twins made their case, and for most of those minutes Lane laughed. He promised them he would get back to them.

"So you're plan B!" April said throwing her hands up. "Those little heifers think they can go over my head!"

"Babe, it's okay. They are just excited."

April rolled her eyes, pouting. "Lord only knows what they have cooked up with my gullible Daddy."

Lane was laughing. "Just tell me where to be, what time and what to write the check for!" "Thanks for being so easy about this," April said very softly. He winked at her.

Chapter 42

Symphony was startled for a second waking up in Grant's arms. They were both completely naked. He was sleeping soundly, and snoring slightly. She just laid there, and watched him. "Oh my gosh," she thought, we got married. This is insane! Grant, wake up," she whispered in his ear. He squirmed, but didn't open his eyes. Symphony leaned up on one elbow, and kissed his lips. He opened his eyes, looked at her for a long moment, then said, "Hello wife."

Their eyes locked, "I thought maybe you forgot."

"Forgot, I married you? No way." He pulled her into his arms again and held her tight, eventually pulling her on top of him.

When they finally got up they had brunch, and talked about important things like telling their families they were married, where they would live, and dealing with Sunny.

After brunch they went to the magistrate's office, got the marriage license, and took it to the Chaplin to be signed. With all that taken care of, Symphony asked to see Grant's apartment. He laughed, and pretended to talk her out of it.

The apartment was neat, and the proverbial bachelor pad. Symphony found something familiar about it. It smelled like Grant. It was warm like him. She looked around, mentally prepared to see a picture of Sunny. The only pictures were of his family; his parents and sister.

"Do you think your sister will like me?" Symphony asked Grant.

"Where did that come from?" Grant answered laughing.

"My friends who have significant others with sisters say they are harder to deal with than mothers."

"That's probably true and Gretchen may be standoffish initially, but she will warm up to you."

He put his arms around her, and kissed the back of her neck.

"When are we going to Charlotte?" Symphony asked. "Next weekend, then we'll fly to Shreveport."

"Let's plan something soon to get both families together in Charlotte. I'm sure my parents won't mind, since your dad can't travel. "

He smiled at her. "Thanks for being considerate of him.

"Of course. I hate to go back to Virginia Beach tomorrow," Symphony said.

"I hate for you to go, but I'm coming back there Friday as soon as I finish with my last patient," Grant said. "I wish I could drive you back tomorrow."

"I'm good with the drive. Three hours on the road, I can listen to the lecture I missed today, and a Japanese module!"

Grant wrapped his arms around her, and they shared a passionate kiss.

"Can we stay here tonight?" Symphony asked.

"Are you sure?"

"Yes, I want to be in your bed."

"Okay, let's go back to the hotel and get our stuff," he said.

"Let's get some food, and cook tonight," she said walking in the kitchen and opening the refrigerator and cabinets.

Just as they stopped at the traffic light outside the resident's gate, Sunny turned in front of Grant's car and slammed on brakes.

Chapter 43

"To what do I owe the pleasure of a call from the incomparable Coach Sterling Chance?" Carissa Jade was a radio personality on a sports satellite radio station. She was also a woman who liked drama, especially if she created it. Carissa was Sterling's cousin's cousin, and they were friends from childhood. Being mixed race, with a black father and white mother, her hair was dark blond, but curly, and her eyes were light brown. Sterling always thought she was beautiful, smart and a bit too much. He had a secret crush on her for years. But he also knew if you needed somebody in a fight with you, she was the one.

After a few minutes to catch up, Sterling told Carissa he needed her help.

"What's going on baby?" Carissa asked seriously.

"I need your help, and this is a huge favor." Sterling's voice was serious, almost sad.

"Talk to me Sterling."

Very carefully, almost methodically, he explained the situation with Kathy. He admitted coaxing Kathy into having sex, with the goal of eventually getting her pregnant. He told Carissa the condom "broke." He didn't tell her he pricked it with a pin to cause the break.

Carissa listened intently, quite amazed at the circumstances, and was also amused that Kathy was willing to walk away from a man like Sterling, who obviously loved her very much.

"I want you to be my live in love interest, to portray my girl, and the baby's intended other parent."

"Because you know Kathy, like most women, don't want another woman raising her kid," Carissa said with a slight laugh.

"Precisely!" Sterling responded not laughing.

They talked a while, put a plan in place with a timeline. "We need to be seen together in some public places, and eventually in some private settings," Carissa offered.

"We need to move quickly, we only have seven months, and the baby will be here."

"Okay, can you go to a charity event with me Thursday night?"

"Yep, I'll make it work," Sterling said.

Kathy found her things in the foyer of her parents' home the next morning. She had a headache from not sleeping, and a lump in her throat from crying. She was pregnant and didn't want to be, the man she loved hated her, and her parents were disappointed in her. What a life.

Walking through the house, Kathy realized no one else was there. Her mother would be back shortly for lunch and to take her to the airport.

Kathy threw the rest of her things in a bag, and called a car to go to the airport. Riding with her mother wasn't what she wanted to do. Once back in New York she could get her bearings. Kathy never thought being away from home, away from Hattiesville, would give her more peace than being there.

On the ride to the airport, Kathy received a text message from Sterling. He simply asked how she felt, and asked her to let him know when she was back in New York City. While waiting to board her flight, Katherine called and let Kathy know in no uncertain terms she didn't appreciate her leaving without any explanation, and didn't appreciate her attitude.

"Mama, I don't have the mental or physical energy to do this with you right now. I will let you know when I get back home."

Katherine didn't like Kathy calling New York home.

The flight to LaGuardia airport from Charlotte was a little less than two hours, just enough time for a nap.

Chapter 44

Jacksa had been back at work for a week when her Bureau phone signaled she had a message. The text message indicated a time and number to call.

Three days after Andre and Jacksa completed the sale of the Corvette, the bureau implemented their planned raid. Unbeknownst to Jacksa, Anderson was back in the states, and running the operation.

The raid was simultaneous at three locations; the garage, Andre's home, and the home of his boss. The local police, and the bureau exchanged gunfire at the boss's house, and an officer got winged, but the suspect was taken in. Andre was arrested without incident, but there was a major situation at the garage.

The bureau agents and local police silently converged on the garage. They surrounded the building then hit the sirens, and flood lights. Gun fire erupted almost immediately.

The men inside the garage had high powered artillery, and there were more of them than Cutter and the Bureau were aware of. Two officers were hit, four of Andre's co-

conspirators were hit, one fatally, and the car was hit. When all was said and done, the arrests made, Cutter and another agent examined the car with Anderson on the phone. They carefully took out the seats, went through the glove compartment, and the center console. There were guns in the trunk and drugs hidden under the carpet. There was money and a watch in the console.

"Check the headlights man!" Anderson said for the second time.

"Chill man," Cutter responded, "we are doing this strictly by the book. I'm waiting on the photographer to finish phase one of his report."

The photographer and tech joined them shortly after Cutter's comment. The tech carefully removed the driver's side headlight. Something fell to the floor. They thought it was glass from the shattered windshield. It was a diamond. "What the hell?" Cutter asked. He picked up the sparkling particle and held it to the camera. "Man that's why he said the headlights were worth so much!"

"Exactly!" Anderson shouted.

Upon close inspection there were more diamonds, as well as cocaine, and cash. More of the same behind the headlight on the other side. The crime scene agents took over, practically disassembled the car and catalogued everything they found.

Hours later, Cutter signed off on everything, including Anderson being able to go home. Late that night, he boarded a flight from Minneapolis to Charlotte. Wendy Wolfe picked him up, and took him to Jacksa's house.

The call Jacksa made indicated the time she should be at home and available for follow up from Wendy. The follow up was Anderson; home and free of the criminals who wanted him dead. Other than Jacksa's dog Pepper growling and snapping at him, it was a good homecoming. Jacksa left him in bed the next morning. He slept most of the day.

When she was home from work that evening, Anderson had cooked dinner, and while they ate, he wanted to talk about three things; going to see his Grandmother, mothers and sisters, going to see her parents, and getting married. Quickly they decided to see her parents the next day, and go to Catawba to see his family on Saturday. They would spend the night with Honey.

Jacksa still wore her engagement ring, but Anderson wanted to upgrade it. She said no. "This ring was a comfort to me during the worse time of my life; when I didn't know if you were dead or alive. I never want to part with it." He decided to have an extraordinary band created with the diamonds from his grandmother's ring.

They also decided not to wait and plan a wedding. Anderson needed to talk to Bishop Robinson anyway, and when he did he would ask how soon the Bishop could marry them. After their honeymoon he would go back to work. Anderson was curious to see what his next assignment would be.

Chapter 45

"Damnit!" Grant shouted. "Are you okay?" he asked Symphony.

"Yes, I'm fine."

Grant got out of the car, and so did Sunny, running toward him shouting.

"Where have you been? Why haven't you answered my calls?"

Symphony sat there deciding whether to get out of the car. She looked at Grant, but he was looking at Sunny. Symphony quickly sized her up; attractive, with expensive taste based on her outfit and accessories, and her car, and obviously a little crazy.

A military police officer pulled up on a golf cart. He saluted Grant, and asked if everything was alright. When Grant responded that it was, he asked them to move away from the exit. Sunny looked exasperated, but they didn't have a choice. Walking back to her car, Sunny looked back at Grant twice. Getting back into his car he said to Symphony, "I didn't intend to deal with her today, but here we go." She reached for his hand, and held it while he drove down the block behind Sunny to a parking lot. Once he parked, he kissed the back of Symphony's hand, and told her to "Come on." By the time he walked around the car to open her door, Sunny was standing right beside him. Holding Symphony's hand, Grant said to Sunny, "this is Symphony Sturdivant, my wife. Symphony this is Sunny Durant, my ex." Sunny cringed at the word "ex."

Neither of the ladies acknowledged the other. Turning to face Grant, Sunny said, "Your wife! Are you freakin' kiddin' me?"

"No. Symphony and I got married Sunday," he said calmly.

"When did you meet her, Saturday?"

Symphony and Grant looked at one another and smiled. Sunny started firing questions at Grant and calling him names. Her Bahamian accent kicked in, and she even pushed him. Sunny was crying, and Symphony was embarrassed for her. Grant let go of Symphony's hand, to defend Sunny's blows. He finally stepped back, and she lost her balance, stumbling slightly. She recovered quickly, and lowered her voice a bit. "We were together a few weeks ago, and you just walk away…"

Grant cut her off. "Sunny we were done before you went home for the funeral. I saw you when you came back to be supportive, not for any other reason."

The hurt was evident on her face.

"I'm not telling you anything you didn't already know. The last time I saw you, when you went through my phone, I told you again we were over."

Then it dawned on Sunny. This was the woman he met at the beach when they were there for New Years. She turned to Symphony, "So you are the one who ruined my vacation, and kept him from moving back in with me when we got back to D.C."

"No Sunny, you ruined your relationship with Grant. Not me." Symphony said.

"Shut up. You don't know me or anything about my relationship with Grant…"

Symphony interrupted her. "What I do know is, Grant is my husband."

Sunny just looked at her. On his way around the car to open the door for Symphony, Grant stopped between Sunny and Symphony. He looked at Sunny. "Get yourself together Sunny. Treat people the way you want to be treated." Symphony got in the car, but kept her eyes on Sunny. "And respect my marriage," Grant said as he closed the car door. They drove off and left Sunny standing there.

"Sweetie, unfortunately we probably haven't heard the last of Sunny," Grant said holding Symphony's hand.

"Most likely you're right. You just be careful. Keep your eyes open."

"I will be fine. I know her," Grant said.

At the hotel, they got everything to go back to Grant's apartment. When they were in the grocery store, Grant looked around. Symphony was right, he had to be aware of his surroundings. He didn't put anything pass Sunny.

They had a good evening. Sunny didn't call or text. At one-point Grant thought about the crazy women who had been in his life; Janis and Sunny. He was never going to marry Janis, but he was glad he dodged the "Sunny bullet."

Chapter 46

The call came very early in the morning. There was a horrible accident with a number of casualties, and all available medical personnel were asked to report to the hospital. Lane got up, hurried to get in the shower. April went to the kitchen to fix him a sandwich. When he walked in dressed in sweats, April remarked how good he looked. "Don't make me lose my focus girl," he said to her laughing. His phone rang. "Hey Belinda. Yeah I did. I need you in my O.R. I don't know what we're up against, and I'm not in the mood to bring anybody up to speed."

April's sister Belinda only worked on call. She was an excellent scrub nurse, and also the mother of four children. But when Lane called Belinda usually tried to accommodate him. "Tell Belinda to let me know if I need to help with the kids," April said. "I will. I'll call you later." A quick kiss, and he was out the door. On the drive to the hospital, Lane thought about April, and how much he appreciated her support. Not lost on him was the information he knew she had from Tamara. His only hope was she thought Tamara was jealous, or trying to get back at him.

Lane and Belinda had a horrific day. Two of the three patients they operated on died. One of them was a teenager, which hit Lane particularly hard. He went to his office, and fell onto the couch. After a few compound curse words, he went to his desk, opened the bottom drawer and pulled out an open bottle of vodka and a shot glass. He drank one shot, then another, then another, until it was all gone.

The knock at the door didn't awaken him. When he didn't answer she knocked again. Easing the door open, Belinda called his name before walking in.

Lane was on the couch lying on his back. His mouth was open, he was drooling, and snoring. The empty vodka bottle was on the desk. The glass still in his hand. Belinda looked over her shoulder to make sure nobody was behind her. She walked all the way in, and locked the door.

Lane. Lane!" Belinda shook his shoulder. He looked up at her squinting, and wiping his mouth with the back of his hand. Sitting up slowly, he held his head in both hands. Neither of them said anything for a long moment. Finally, Belinda sat in a chair opposite him. "What in the world is going on with you?" He cleared his throat, contemplating what to say to her, quickly realizing lying to her was pointless.

"Belinda, losing that kid was like a punch in the gut. I lost it when I got in here."

His speech was slurred, and he was obviously still trying to get his eyes to focus. She didn't take her eyes off him, and he knew she was serious. Belinda got up, went to the credenza and poured him a glass of water. Handing it to him, she said in a forceful tone, "You have lost patients before, and I know for a fact you didn't drink to the point you passed out."

Lane took a long drink of water. "Belinda, I used to drink too much. I'm not an alcoholic, I didn't go to treatment, I stopped on my own. Until today I hadn't had a drink at all in months. That's probably why having a couple knocked me out. Plus, Belinda; I'm exhausted." Lane hoped she understood, or at the very least, accepted his explanation.

"Does April know about the drinking problem?"

"It's not a problem," he said a little too defensively."

"Does April know you were drinking too much?" Belinda used her fingers to make quote signs. Lane sighed loudly, and wiped his face with both hands. "Unfortunately, we had an instance when I overacted to something because of the alcohol. That was the last time I had anything to drink." Lane sounded better, his eyes were focused, and clear, but his mouth was dry. In college they called it "cotton mouth". Clearing his throat, he continued. "Don't mention this to April. Let me take care of it. I don't want her to worry unnecessarily."

"Don't act like this isn't serious Lane. It is. Do you know the ramifications if somebody other than me had come in here?"

"Yeah Belinda. I do. Glad that didn't happen." He stood.

"Lane, April needs to know about this, and she needs to know that I know. If she doesn't mention it to me in a couple days, I will ask her about it." Belinda's voice was firm, but the look on her face was unyielding. He didn't underestimate her or her influence on April. Belinda was the one who introduced Lane and April, and he knew Belinda could undo it too.

Chapter 47

The event Carissa invited Sterling to was well attended, and people were there who needed to see them together. Both being local celebrities they got a lot of attention. Two people who were at the Christmas party when Sterling proposed to Kathy did inquire about her absence. One asked directly; why as an engaged man was he at the event with "a woman like Carissa." To which he responded, "I am not an engaged man anymore." She was stunned, and wasn't able to respond before he walked away.

Carissa played her part to the max. Sterling was amazed at how much she understood what he needed. She was good for him. He couldn't have paid for a better performance.

"Thank you for winning the bid for me. I love this bag!" Carissa was admiring the designer overnight bag Sterling won in the silent auction. He laughed. He was driving Carissa home.

"Do you want to spend the night?"

The question caught Sterling off guard. "Naw. Not tonight. I have an early weight training class."

"We need to leave home together in the mornings," Carissa said.

"Yeah, I know, but we don't want to look like I was seeing you while Kathy and I were together." Sterling said quietly.

"You're right. I don't mean to get in front of your plan and process. I just want Kathy to have a reality check."

"I'm not sure I have a plan or a process."

"But the point is, you love her, and she is blowing it. I have only ever imagined being with a man like you. A good dude who is honorable, and about his situation. I can't believe she is walking away from you. And her kid! I'll probably never have kids!"

"Why do you think you won't have a husband and kids?" Sterling looked over at Carissa frowning.

"Nobody takes me seriously." Carissa answered.

"What does that mean?"

"Honestly because of what I do. Because I talk so much trash on the air, and because I know so much about sports, most men see me as 'one of the guys'! And nobody believes Carissa Jade is my real name!"

Sterling laughed a loud belly laugh. "It does sound like a stripper's name," he said still laughing.

She punched his arm with her fist. He kept laughing.

"Any man who can see knows you're not one of the boys."

Carissa blushed.

Sterling walked Carissa to her door. She put her arms around his waist. He kissed her forehead. It was a tender moment between them. "Thank you," Sterling said to Carissa. "I couldn't trust everybody with this."

"Thank you for trusting me," she said with a light in her eyes.

"Sterling has moved on."

"What are you talking about Kat?" Lee asked Katherine.

"Sterling was at the Sickle Cell fundraiser with a date."

"And I'm sure one of your gossiping friends told you that."

"Does it matter who told me? The point is the father of our grandchild is already involved with another woman." Katherine paused waiting for Lee to comment. He didn't. "Kathy needs to know. Maybe that will jolt her back into reality," Katherine continued.

"Love, Sterling was at the benefit with Carissa Jade, the sports commentator. She does sports, he's a coach, sounds like colleagues at an event to me."

"Why do you know that?" Katherine looked at him blankly.

"I have gossiping friends too!" They both laughed.

Lee wanted Katherine to leave Kathy and Sterling alone. He felt confident they would work it out, and they didn't need her influence.

Back in her New York apartment, Kathy took her mind off her current circumstances and focused on the week ahead. She was eager to get back to class and studying, and even her duties as a research assistant. Briefly she entertained not being able to keep up that schedule for the whole semester. In the midst of the same contemplation she reminded herself the course she missed could be made up with an online class during the summer. Shifting her thoughts back to the tasks at hand, the phone rang. Kathy immediately realized she didn't let Sterling know she was back. But the caller was her cousin Michelle. Taking a deep breath, she answered, trying hard to sound cheerful.

Michelle didn't waste any time on formalities or being courteous. Her voice was quiet, almost sad. "I talked with Aunt Kat, and I know you're giving the baby to Sterling." Kathy didn't immediately respond. "Why Kathy?"

"I'm not giving the baby to Sterling, he will just be the primary caregiver..."

"The custodial parent," Michelle said, "With the right to call the shots." Michelle made it sound awful.

"It's the best arrangement for the baby. I've given this a lot of thought. Sterling is settled, he has the money to hire a sitter, or a nanny. I don't know where I'll end up living. The baby should be close to my parents too."

"Aunt Kat said Sterling told you to expect to give up your rights."

"'Chelle, Sterling did say that, but he didn't mean it. He was angry, and lashing out at me. He's a reasonable man. He won't ask me to give up my rights," Kathy said confidently.

"I pray you're right."

Neither of them said anything for a few seconds. Michelle broke the silence. "You know football coaches go to other schools in other cities. DavisTown is a good school with a small program. Sterling has worked hard and you best believe a big school maybe even the pros are going to call him." Michelle paused. Kathy still didn't respond so Michelle started talking again. "Your baby could grow up in Phoenix or Seattle; away from you, your parents and me."

"I don't know what to say. I know you don't get it…"

"No I don't. I think you're selfish!" Michelle said.

"You're entitled to your opinion," Kathy said as her phone beeped. It was Sterling. "' Chelle I need to go. Sterling is calling." Not waiting for Michelle to respond, Kathy disconnected the call.

"Hi Sterling."

"Hey Kathy. How are you?" He sounded so formal, and she was unaccustomed to him using her name, and not one of his pet names for her.

"I'm good! How are you?"

"I'm cool. How was your flight?"

"Everything was good. I'm getting planned for the week," she said again determined to sound cheerful.

"What did you eat?"

She answered him.

"How are you getting to school in the morning?

She answered. The question and answer dialogue went for a couple minutes more. Sterling ended the call, and Kathy cried.

Chapter 48

"What the hell Grant?" You did what? Married who?"

Gretchen was screaming at Grant. He held the phone away from his ear and Symphony could hear her clearly. Both hands covered her mouth.

"GG, you are going to love Symphony," he said evenly. There was a weighty silence between them. Grant finally said to his sister, "We're coming next weekend, can you get my room ready, and make me some banana bread?" He looked at Symphony, winked and smiled.

"Yes Grant. Yes. You are always thinking about your damn stomach," Gretchen said. He knew he had her.

The next call to his parents wasn't as dramatic, but they were nonetheless shocked. Grace asked if Symphony was pregnant. "No Ma, she's not. Real talk."

Paul simply congratulated his son, and said "we'll talk when you and your bride get here."

"Yes sir." Grant knew he meant it.

Symphony's call to her parents was intense, but not severe. Her mother's concern the same as Grace's. "Mama, I promise I'm not pregnant," she looked at Grant and shrugged.

"Not yet!" He whispered. Symphony rolled her eyes.

"We're going to Charlotte next weekend, and we're coming to Shreveport, the following weekend," Symphony was talking to her dad. "Umm, okay. Let me talk to your mother, we may meet you in North Carolina." Symphony was surprised, she looked at Grant, wide eyed. Her father was still talking. "We may as well meet his family."

"Okay, Daddy, just let me know."

"I will Sunshine. Love you."

"Love you!" She knew he would be okay when he called her Sunshine.

As soon as they hung up, Symphony told Grant what her Dad said.

"That works for me."

"I think it's going to be too much! I don't think I can handle meeting your family and having them meet my parents at the same time."

"Sure you can. I got you." He put his arms around her.

On Monday, Symphony's mother called to tell her they would meet them in Charlotte on Friday. "Ask Grant to let us know of a hotel in Charlotte close to his parents' home."

"We'll take care of making a reservation for you," Symphony told her mother.

"Darling where are you living? What are you doing about your classes and your internship?"

Symphony sat, and explained to her mother the arrangements she and Grant made.

"His schedule is pretty flexible, and I don't have a class on Friday so it works for us to alternate weekends. We are committed to do it this way until May when I graduate. Then I'll move to D.C., which will actually give me good job options. We haven't talked about the internship.

"So you all really have thought this through," her mother said.

"Yes, Ma! We spend a lot of time on the phone!"

"You have always made practical decisions and this impromptu marriage seems so out of character for you."

"I know, and I can't make you understand, but in my heart of hearts this feels right."

Gretchen called Grant at work. She needed to talk with him alone. He wasn't surprised his sister called. Gretchen had calmed considerably. Grant told her about his and

Symphony's weekend together, that prompted him to propose.

"Did you ever consider she may have said no and thought you were crazy?" Gretchen asked seriously.

"No I didn't consider she would think I was crazy, but the thought did cross my mind that she may say no," Grant responded just as seriously. Before she could bring it up, Grant told his sister about the encounter with Sunny.

"Do you think she will just walk away."

"Nooo, not at all. I expect her around every corner."

"Does Symphony…."

Grant anticipated Gretchen's question. "Yep. I told her about me and Sunny, and our challenges." He laughed, and continued. "I was with Sunny when I met Symphony."

He went on to explain.

"Grant that's not funny. That's nasty."

Grant really laughed.

"I wouldn't have said anything to you…checking in a hotel with one woman, and trying to talk to me!"

"And that's why you are single! Lookin' for a perfect situation."

Chapter 49

Lane called April on his way to her house, to see what she wanted to eat. Along with the grocery order, he bought a bouquet of flowers.

April knew Lane had something on his mind the moment he walked in. He gave her the flowers, hugged her tightly, and then went to the shower. She didn't say anything, just went to the kitchen.

While they ate, Lane told her about the patients, and the surgeries, and the young patient who died. She noticed how sad and defeated he sounded. Not really knowing what to say, she just listened. While they cleaned the kitchen, they talked about other things; including having children, and how soon they would start a family. April was saying wait two years, and have two kids back to back.

"Do you know if the twin gene is on your dad's side or Belinda's mom's side of the family?" Lane asked.

April laughed before she answered. "We don't know. Of course Belinda doesn't know anything about her biological mother, and we don't know of any other twins on the Josephs side."

"So you may be the test case." Lane looked at April very seriously, but didn't say anything.

"Dr. Silver, if that is your professional opinion, you can keep it to yourself!" They both laughed. "One baby at a time," April said.

"Babe, what's the difference between having two babies and having a second one nine or ten months after the first one?"

"Probably nothing, but saying that just makes me feel better."

Lane knew he had prolonged the conversation they really needed to have. He took her hand and walked to the sofa. April took a deep breath. She knew what that meant. He needed to talk about something serious. Pulling her into his arms he held her tightly. She relaxed a bit, thinking maybe talking wasn't on his mind. But then he spoke just above a whisper.

"Something else happened today, after surgery. I went to my office, had a…had several drinks and passed out. Belinda found me." April didn't comment. She was looking at Lane but her face was soft. He continued. "Sweetie, before I moved here, I was drinking too much. I'm not an alcoholic. I didn't go to treatment. I just stopped drinking." April thought about Tamara telling her he missed a surgery. Like he was reading her mind, he said, "I stopped when I slept through a surgery one morning." Her body language changed because he kissed her cheek, and snuggled closer. April remained silent. "And, I know you and Tamara talked."

"How do you know that?" Those were the first words out of her mouth.

"She called me."

"I didn't think you and Tamara were still in touch." April said, unwrapping herself from his arms.

"April we aren't. I was surprised to see her at the wedding. We didn't even speak, so I was absolutely surprised to get the call. I thought somebody was dead." Her shoulders relaxed so he pulled her back into his arms, as he continued. "I told Tam she had no right to discuss any of that with you. It wasn't her story to tell. As I shared with you, we had a set of challenges that went far beyond my drinking."

Speaking softly April said to Lane, "she told me about an incident when you got aggressive with her like you did with me."

"That did happen." He paused, neither of them saying anything for a few seconds. "April, until today I hadn't had a drop of alcohol since that night. Wait...I had champagne at the wedding."

"So what's your plan to deal with the situation?" April asked, but it was more a demand for action.

Lane didn't answer immediately. Kissing both her hands he finally said, "I don't need a plan. I'm not drinking, and I won't start again. I can do it on my own."

April didn't respond right away. Removing her hands from his, she clasped her fingers together covering her mouth. She bowed her head as if in prayer, closing her eyes for a few moments. She looked up, saying very matter-of-factly, "I won't marry you if you don't get professional help."

Lane swallowed hard, but didn't miss a beat. "I will call the employee assistance agency first thing in the morning."

April smiled slightly. Lane kissed her forehead. She exhaled.

"One last thing," he said. April lifted her head. "Let Belinda know we talked."

"Because my big sister threatened to tell me if you didn't."

"Yes, but understand she only has your best interest at heart."

"I'll call her tomorrow," April said laying her head on Lane's shoulder.

Chapter 50

Sunny cried until her head hurt. Grant said he married Symphony. "Why would he rather marry her than me?" She thought. "Grant doesn't get it. My friends are going to laugh me out of town. I have to do something to get his attention." Her phone rang and interrupted her thoughts. It was her mother.

"What is wrong wit you gal? Move on. People break up eryday. That's how life is," her mother said.

"Mama you don't understand."

"Yeah, I do. I understand you made him secon' to you, to the weddin' and to impressin' you friens."

Sunny started crying again. "Wipe yo teahs. Ya betta then dat. Ya bounce back soon."

"Mama, he got married," Sunny said between sniffles.

"I hear you chile. I don like it, but dats up to him. Men do dum' stuff. If he that impulsive ya don need 'im anyway."

There was no consoling her, so Sunny's mother ended the call.

"Symphony! What is all this stuff?" Grant was frowning.

"All the stuff I need to cook for your dad!"

"Girl we have grocery stores in Charlotte."

"That's true husband, but I'm not familiar with them, and I can't mess this up."

He loved the sound of her saying, "husband". Grant loaded the coolers full of seafood and ice into the back of his SUV, and put their luggage on the floor in the back seat.

Not running into more than the normal amount of traffic, they arrived in Charlotte on schedule. Symphony received a text from her mother saying they were on the ground in Charlotte, and she would let them know when they were at the hotel.

They were both a little nervous. Exiting the interstate, Symphony exhaled. Grant reached over and took her hand, holding it until they were in his parent's driveway. Gretchen's car wasn't there. That was fine with Grant. He preferred to deal with her separately. He knew she would overtake the conversation with his parents and he wanted them to meet Symphony without the drama his sister could bring.

Opening Symphony's door, Grant kissed her lips lightly, and grabbed her hand. Grace opened the door before they reached the porch. She was smiling.

"Hey Ma."

"Hey darling." They stepped inside.

"Ma, this is Symphony!"

"Hello Mrs. Sturdivant…"

Grace hugged her. "It's my pleasure to meet you." Grant was smiling. Symphony had tears in her eyes. Grace's smile was genuine; her hug was warm. "You are more beautiful in person than the picture Grant sent me." Symphony smiled, and looked at Grant, who winked at her.

"Gracie, let her go," Paul, Grant's father said.

"Daddy, my beautiful bride, Symphony."

Paul reached up with both arms. Symphony leaned down into his embrace.

"Move girl, don't try to butter up my daddy." They all laughed.

"Come on in," Paul said turning his wheelchair around.

"I need to get the coolers out the car," Grant said.

"What's in the coolers?"

Symphony answered Paul. "I brought you some seafood, and I'm going to cook for you tomorrow."

"Well alright! Let's me and you go back here and talk about that," Paul said. Symphony followed him.

Grace and Grant had a few minutes alone. They hugged. "I have a good feeling about her son."

"She's amazing Ma." Before he could say anything else he heard a car. It was Gretchen.

"Ma, please don't let GG act up."

"Your sister is fine. No more surprised than the rest of us. She's just more verbal. You know how protective she is of you."

"I know," Grant said with a sigh.

Grant met Gretchen in the driveway. They hugged. "Help me get this stuff out the truck."

"I'm not," she said, and pouted. "What is all that anyway?" Gretchen followed him inside with the larger cooler explaining what was in it.

"Hey Ma, hey Da." Her parents spoke and then Gretchen introduced herself to Symphony. She didn't hug Symphony, but she did smile.

"Nice to meet you Gretchen. Grant told me you two look alike, but he didn't say how much!" Symphony smiled. Gretchen looked over her shoulder at Grant and rolled her eyes.

"Let me help you with that," Grace said to Grant, opening the door to the garage. "Let's put that stuff in the refrigerator out here."

"Are your parents here yet?" Paul asked Symphony.

"Yes sir. Grant said they are about five minutes from here."

When Grant and Grace came back into the house the conversation moved to getting the Sandhurst's there for dinner.

"What did you cook?" Grant asked his sister.

"What difference does it make?" You're going to eat it anyway! She replied sarcastically. They started fussing. "Can you two please call a truce for the weekend? You're going to make Symphony not want to be here," Grace said laughing.

"Too late sister-in-law. You're stuck. You shoulda asked me before you married this knucklehead. No turning back now," Gretchen said as she pushed Grant's head with her finger, and walked into the other room. Grant smiled.

Symphony's parents offered to get a car and come to the Sturdivant's, but Symphony and Grant agreed meeting the whole family at the same time would be a bit much. They drove to the hotel, Grant on the other side of the situation now.

"You don't think your daddy is going to shoot me or anything do you?"

"Maybe just in the knee!"

Grant had to laugh.

Colonel Richmond Sandhurst opened the door to the suite. Symphony practically jumped in his arms. About the time the door closed, her mother walked into the sitting area. Holding her dad's hand, Symphony said, "Daddy, Mama, this is my amazing husband Grant Sturdivant."

Grant waited for Richmond to extend his hand, and unknowingly standing at attention, shook it firmly. Alicia Sandhurst took the couple of steps forward and hugged Grant. It was a real hug. The four of them moved out of the foyer to the sitting area.
"Thanks Sweetie. This is a lovely suite," Symphony's mother said.

"You're welcome," Grant said and they all laughed.

"Membership has its privileges," Symphony said.

Grant decided to go on offense. He looked directly at Richmond. "Sir, I know this is not how you expected to meet your son-in-law, but please trust me. I love Symphony and I will do right by her, take good care of her."

"Thanks for saying that Grant. You're correct, the situation is unusual, but I know my daughter. If she married you, and didn't talk to me about it, you are damn near perfect. Be clear, Symphony is my only child, and I will protect her with my life." Richmond was looking Grant straight in the eyes with no hint of a smile.

"Yes sir. I am very clear. I get it. I have a sister, I'm sure my dad feels the same way about her."

"You have a twin sister, is that right?" Alicia asked to lighten the mood.

"Yes ma'am. Her name is Gretchen. I call her GG. You'll meet her tonight."

"Why don't we head back to the Sturdivant's," Symphony said standing. "Gretchen and Mrs. Sturdivant cooked dinner for us."

On the short drive back to his parents' home, Grant told the Sandhurts about his dad's injury.

"That's horrific, but sounds like he's doing well under the circumstances," Alicia said.

"He's great Ma!" Symphony said.

At the house introductions were easy, and conversations went smoothly. A spectator wouldn't think they all just met.

The men migrated to the den to watch a basketball game, and the ladies finished the kitchen and settled in the dining room. Grant felt his phone vibrate. Anybody who would call him was there with him. He started to ignore it, but then thought better of it. Stepping out of the room to answer. Grant was surprised when the caller identified herself as an ER nurse at Howard University Hospital.

"What can I do for you? Grant asked, expecting the call to be about a patient.

"Sunny Durant is in our ER, and you are listed as her emergency contact." Before Grant could respond, the caller continued, "She attempted to commit suicide." Grant sighed loudly before he replied to that news.

"Ma'am, Ms. Durant's info needs to be updated. I am no longer her emergency contact. You need to call her mother." For a split second Grant was going to offer her the number to call Sunny's mother, but decided he didn't even want to be that involved. There was a long pause and then the caller thanked Grant and disconnected the call. Grant stood for a moment. That was a stunt. There was no way Sunny would kill herself. Her expectation was that he would run to her rescue. Not this time. Grant went back to the den; his team was down by three points. He didn't share the news with anyone, and didn't intend to ever speak of it.

When Gretchen was ready to leave, she offered to drop the Sandhurst's back at the hotel.

"Thanks Sis," Grant said hugging her. We'll be over in a little while. Daddy and I need to talk for a few minutes.

While Grace showed Symphony pictures of young Grant, he and Paul talked in the den. "Son, Symphony is obviously beautiful, and apparently amazing. With all you've been through, why did you make such a hasty decision?"

Grant paused briefly before he replied. "You're right, she's gorgeous, smart and incredible. And, yep, I've been to hell and back. I didn't think I would survive Leah's death, but I did."

Paul nodded. Grant continued.

"But the sum of my experience; life is short, true love is rare, time ain't on my side, and go with my gut, which tells me this is right."

Chapter 51

It was raining like crazy. "Why don't you stay the night?" Sterling asked Carissa.

"I will if you want me to."

The two of them were in a routine that in the real world would be considered dating. She was at his house tonight after a basketball game at DavisTown College. Because his house was closer they went there for Carissa to file her report with the radio station. Before they knew it, the storm came.

Sterling gave Carissa a t-shirt, and a toothbrush. When he came out of the bathroom, she was in his bed. He got in beside her, and turned out the light. She put her arms around him and laid her head on his chest. He pulled her close. They laid there a minute or two quietly. He put his hands under the t-shirt to find that she was wearing nothing else. Carissa leaned in and kissed him. He responded.

Early the next morning when he awakened, Sterling looked over at Carissa. He couldn't see her well, it was still dark, but he knew she was sleeping soundly. Her breathing even. In his mind, he replayed the night before. Carissa was unbelievable; passionate, unselfish, exciting and had no sexual inhibitions or constraints. Unfairly, he laid there and compared Carissa and Kathy. He didn't have to coax Carissa. And, she knew the extra things to do, the perfume, and the light lip gloss. Kathy was inexperienced, but it was like she had no imagination. Sterling exhaled, as he thought, but "I love Kathy."

"Do we need to talk?" Carissa whispered.

"I guess so." Sterling's response was flat.

"You don't have to feel guilty. I seduced you, and I know that wasn't part of our arrangement," she said.

"I don't feel guilty! At all! I asked you to stay. I wanted you here, and I wanted you in my bed. I wanted to make love to you."

"Love! Sterling there was no love in what we did last night. That was pure sex. If I wasn't a lady, I would use another word! You did everything with me you want to do with her, but you knew she wouldn't let you."

"I don't want you to feel used 'cause that's definitely not the situation."

"What is the 'situation'?" Carissa asked putting emphasis on the word.

Sterling leaned up on his elbow, then said, "the situation is, I asked you to help me make Kathy jealous, so she would come back to me, and be my wife and a mother to our child.

But, I didn't consider the full cost…the fact there's some chemistry between us that I can't – won't deny," he said seriously.

Carissa laughed. "Sterling, I have loved you since I was nine years old. Do you remember we kissed under the…"

"pecan tree," they said in unison…

" in my grandmother's yard."

"Yep! Damn that was a minute ago," Sterling said laughing.

"Yes it was. I was eleven years old. In my mind that day, you had proposed to me." They both laughed. "Then you went to that private school, then college, then to the league, and on to bigger and better," Carissa's voice trailed off.

Sterling shifted in the bed, and pulled Carissa into his arms. They were quiet. It was still raining. "I did okay in school, and excelled on the football field, but I knew that girls like you…"
"What do you mean 'girls like me'?"

"Gorgeous, smart, outgoing, ambitious; you were just too much for me. Everything I heard or knew about you was grand. The guys you dated, the places you worked, the people you know."

"And the drama! Admit it!"

"Okay, and the drama."

"I know you know about the fight in the Bucs locker room, and me breaking off my engagement on the radio."

"Which I thought was a publicity stunt," he interjected.

"No," she responded matter-of-factly. "Sterling, I spent my life fighting for identity, so I worked harder, talked louder, dressed better, and generally created ways to be seen." There was some pain in her voice. "But I'm over all that now. I just want to have a regular life; a husband, couple of kids, a house in the suburbs."

"A soccer mom van?" He laughed.

"No! That's where I draw the line!

"I'm over Vegas, L.A., New York City, Miami, the lights, the action. I'm good right here in DavisTown, North Carolina."

Sterling looked down at Carissa, then kissed her. "Let's make a baby," he said and rolled on top of her.

Chapter 52

"I'm uncomfortable 'cause she's a member of the church," Lane said to Ben.

"I know her pretty well; you can trust her. Her professional integrity demands it," Ben said to his future brother-in-law. "Are you uncomfortable to the point of not proceeding? He asked.

"No. I'm committed to it. I want to marry April, so whatever I have to do I will."

As promised, Lane called to get set up with a counselor. When he told April who the appointment was with, she told him the lady was a member of their church. Lane attended irregularly but a lot of people knew who he was.

The first session went fairly well. They talked about forty minutes, mostly about what constituted an alcoholic. The counselor agreed with Lane that he wasn't an alcoholic, but cautioned him it was easy to cross the line. "You are one drink away from it."

With Lane doing what was asked, April put wedding plans in motion. She took a deep breath, called her nieces and invited them, and their mom to go wedding dress shopping with her. They made three appointments.

The entourage determined quickly that what April thought she wanted didn't look like she imagined once it was on. The third appointment was cancelled. April said yes to a dress at the second boutique. It was perfect. The coloring, the beading, the neckline and the cost were all to her liking. The twins were delighted because they actually chose the dress for her to try on.

Over lunch April shared the plan. "I am going to have a small wedding at church, and a sit down dinner at the country club. And, I would like you two to be my bridesmaids."

"Thank you Aunt April," Briana said.

"That's an honor," Brittani said.

"We'll look for your dresses next week. April turned to Belinda. "Big Sis, will you please be my Matron of Honor?" Belinda didn't answer immediately. April knew she was thinking how much territory they had covered since they met. Three years prior April wanted absolutely nothing to do with Hampton Josephs', "other daughter". Brittani and Briana didn't understand the full depth of the situation, but they knew there was major tension between their mother and her sister early on. They also remembered their mother having a heart attack because of stress related to her relationship with April. They all waited.

"And who's going to wrestle with my boys?" Belinda asked laughing.

In an exasperated tone, Briana shouted, "they can't come to the wedding anyway!"

"We'll find them a sitter! Can you imagine?" Brittani followed up.

"Those are your little brothers you're talking about!" Belinda was laughing with them.

"Yeah, little brothers who walk around getting into stuff..." Briana said.

"...And talk loud," Brittani said. The twins both rolled their eyes.

"Yes Sis, of course. I would be honored to be your Matron of Honor." Belinda squeezed April's hand. "And, I will get a sitter for Bryce and Bradley."

With that being settled. Briana changed the subject. "How much money did G-Pop say you can spend?" She asked.

"Bree!" Brittani covered her face with both hands. "Don't be nosey!"

The conversation moved to possible dates, flowers and food. What's the color scheme?" Briana asked.
"Whatever I find that I like for your dresses, and I will build around that."

"Let's do something exotic," Briana continued.

"What exactly does that mean Bree?" April looked at her niece, puzzled.

"You know, like stripes, or polka dots, or we all wear different colors!"

The other three just looked at her. Very carefully, Belinda said to her more "colorful" daughter, "The wedding should mirror the personality of the bride. April is more conservative than you, so I doubt, we're looking for anything exotic!"

"Well, when I get married, we're going to have fabulous, and exotic rolled into one!" Briana smiled.

Brittani looked at her sister, rolled her eyes. "There is no doubt in any of our minds about that!"

Chapter 53

Anderson and Jacksa were married in a private ceremony on a Friday night in the chapel at Hattiesville Community Church. Jacksa's parents, and her brother, Anderson's grandmother, mother and sisters were there, along with about twenty friends. Cutter and Gia were there, and accompanied them on their honeymoon to Curacao, one of the locations approved by the Bureau. Although the gang was in prison, the Bureau still had Anderson in partial protection. "Standard operating procedure," he told Jacksa.

Jacksa had been so caught up in her situation with Anderson, she didn't really know the state of her parents' marriage since her father's affair with a colleague of her mother's was revealed. They were still together and from all indication sleeping in the same bed again. Min, Jacksa's mother wanted to go to counseling. Jackson resisted, but eventually he gave in. Otherwise Min was going to divorce him. They had supported her together when they thought Anderson was dead, and they were truly glad when they found out he was alive. Min's Multiple Sclerosis wasn't any worse, but she decided to retire, promising Jacksa and

Anderson to babysit for them when the time came. She hoped the grands were coming soon.

Both sides of the family wanted Anderson to leave the bureau. "If you want to stay in law enforcement go back to the police department his mother suggested. If they knew the story in its entirety they wouldn't want him to be in law enforcement at all.

The honeymoon was incredible. The island was beautiful, the weather was great, and having friends along gave Jacksa and Anderson a chance to do some things they wanted to do without leaving the other alone. Together they swam, and snorkeled, went sightseeing, and danced. Individually she and Gia shopped, tried the local cuisine, went to a museum, and toured the local university. Anderson and Cutter went to a baseball game, worked out and tried several water sports. Anderson hadn't felt this relaxed in over a year, and he was glad for the break.

Chapter 54

"My grandma told me not to believe what a man tells you in bed unless he will repeat it out of bed." Carissa told Sterling over a plate of French toast he fixed them.

Between bites he responded, "What are you talking about? My comment about making a baby?"

"Yes."

He took a gulp of his milk, wiped his mouth and took both her hands in his.

"I want us to have a family. Me, you, and our two children."

Carissa swallowed hard. He was looking directly into her eyes. His tone was serious.

"Where did that come from Sterling? You don't love me or want me. You are in love with Kathy. I refuse to be your fall back plan! I agreed to play this game with you temporarily, but I'm not bringing a child into this foolishness!"

"It's probably too late," he replied seriously.

She took a sip of coffee, needing a moment to contemplate what Sterling just said. "You love Kathy not me. I hope it's not too late."

"I love a woman who doesn't love me, doesn't want me or the life I want to build. Carissa, all I want in this world is football and a family. I'm good at football, and I will be good at being a family man. You say you're content being in DavisTown, convince me you won't go to Dallas or Tampa Bay with me if the call comes."

She smiled. "I'm not going to Green Bay or Minneapolis!"

He laughed. I have love for you Carissa. I trust you more than anybody else I know. Otherwise, I wouldn't have told you about this, let alone asked you to do this. Bottom line, Rissa, I'm filing for full custody. Over these couple of months, you have shown me more love, and respect than I deserve. You agreed to perpetrate this scheme with me just because I asked you to. Who does that? Only a ride or die!"

"Sterling you're eulogizing your relationship with Kathy. I'm here to make her jealous. If it works, she'll be your wife and raise her own child."

"Then me, you and Kathy can live like those people on tv. What you call 'em? Sister Wives!" He laughed loudly. Carissa stuck up her middle finger which made him laugh more.

"If I got pregnant last night, and Kathy comes to her senses, then me and my baby…"

"...will be fine. I got you girl."

"No Sterling you don't. It's me or Kathy, not me and Kathy."

Sterling took their plates off the counter. Now he needed a minute.

"In my experience, you can give a rookie a play book and run through the plays in practice, but you don't know what they're going to do until the lights come on. The lights are already on for you Miss Jade." He winked at her.

Carissa tried not to smile, but she did. Neither of them said anything for a minute or two. Finally, Carissa said seriously, "I hope I'm not pregnant."

Communication between Kathy and Sterling changed from daily phone calls to occasional calls and more regular text messages. He was busy, and now in a routine with Carissa. Kathy was busy, but she missed him. She missed him a lot.

Sterling felt his phone vibrate. It was Kathy. He didn't answer, texted her; "*you okay?*"

"*Yes.*"

"*Call you later. At a game loud in here.*" He texted back.

Kathy sighed. Sterling was living his normal life. She was in New York, alone, tired, and it seemed always hungry. Her mother suggested coming home for spring break. She said no initially. The thought of packing and flying made her even more tired. Katherine offered to come to New York, but Kathy didn't want that either. The conversation with her cousin Michelle was basically the same; visiting Michelle in Norfolk, or Michelle coming to New York. Kathy wanted to see Sterling, but he hadn't asked her to come home, and hadn't offered to come see her. The last real conversation they had was a few weeks before. She called to tell him she felt the baby move. He was genuinely excited. By the end of the next day Kathy decided to go home. She needed to see her doctor in Hattiesville anyway.

When the phone rang Sterling expected it to be Carissa calling to see what he wanted to eat. He hit his Bluetooth button, and looked at the screen at the same time. He was surprised.

"Hey Kathy," his voice was non-descript.

"Hi Sterling. How are you?" There was a sing-song tone in her voice.

"Good. You sound happy about something."

"I'm coming home next week, and I want you to go to the doctor with me. She's going to perform an ultra-sound and tell us if the baby is a boy or girl!"

Sterling's heart melted. "It's a boy. I'm sure of it."

She laughed. They discussed the details and hung up. Carissa called twice while he was talking to Kathy, but he didn't hear the beep. He was still holding the phone when it rang again.

"What's up?"

"I have a flat tire!
"Where are you?"

"Around the corner from my house."

"You need me to come over there? Sterling asked Carissa.

"Naw, I'm fine. Road side assistance is here, but I have to get a tire in the morning, so I'm going to stay at my house tonight."

Sterling wasn't sure how he felt about that. On one hand he wanted to be alone, to think about Kathy, the baby; his son or his daughter. On the other hand, he wanted and needed to talk about this with Carissa.

"There's no food at your house," he said to Carissa.

"I will pop some popcorn. I'm tired and pissed off about this tire thing."

"Okay. Call me later."

He hung up because his emotions were getting the best of him. An hour later he was at Carissa's door with food.

Kathy felt good about her conversation with Sterling. Better than she had in weeks, and now was looking forward to going home. She called Michelle and asked her to come to Hattiesville. Michelle declined, saying she couldn't get the days off. Hesitantly Kathy called her parents.

"Oh darling, when you said you weren't coming we decided to go to Landridge to see Ben, Belinda and the kids, and visit the church there," her mother said.

Her ace in the hole; "I thought you would want to know if the baby is a boy or girl," Kathy said.

"I do! When is your appointment?"

"Tuesday morning," Kathy was laughing.

"I'll tell your Dad we can't leave until Wednesday."

There was silence between them for a moment. "Kathy is Sterling coming?"

"Yes, he's coming."

Katherine and Sterling had not talked since the night Kathy told her and Lee about the baby. They concocted this scheme that had absolutely backfired. It was her idea, and now Katherine didn't know what to say to Sterling. She would just have to face the music.

Sterling walked in and could smell the burned popcorn. "What are you doing here?" Carissa screamed at him.

"I need you Rissa."

"Why is this about your needs Sterling?"

"Why you mad at me?" He asked.
She started crying. For a minute or two he held her. He repeated the question.

"What I do?" Why you mad at me?"

"Because Sterling. Because!"

He just looked at her and frowned. She was ruffling her thick blond hair with both hands, and biting her bottom lip. All she wore were leggings and a t-shirt.

"Because what?"

"Because you like me, wanna take care of me, treat me good, care about me, and wanna give me a baby. And then I burned the popcorn and you brought me food."

"What's the problem?" Sterling asked.

"The problem is I don't know what to do about it. If the plan works you will be out of my life in a few months."

"Let me tell you what's gettin' ready to happen," he said.

Sterling explained, Kathy was coming home for her break, and would find out the sex of the baby.

"So I'll go with you to the appointment. That will force her hand. She will fall back into your arms, and you will live happily ever after," Carissa said, sucking hard on her straw, making a loud slurping noise with the ice in the bottom of the cup.

"That's not funny Carissa."

"I'm not laughing Sterling."

For a full minute they stared at each other, saying nothing. Sterling dropped his head finally, then got up, walked behind Carissa and wrapped his arms around her. He kissed the back of her neck. She didn't respond. He took her hand and walked to the sofa.

"Hear me clearly. When we see Kathy at the doctor, I will tell her you are my future, and you and I are going to raise the baby. I intended to tell you this later, but I already talked to an attorney about full custody, and …" Sterling paused. He took a deep breath. "I bought you this."

Chapter 55

Sunny took a taxi home from the hospital. She was numb. A seventy-two-hour psych hold. Grant wouldn't come get her, and her mother was in town. She braced herself for the lecture that was coming. Her mother spared her during the hospital stay, but made it abundantly clear they would talk when she got home.

Taking a deep breath, Sunny walked in, and could smell food cooking. The aroma was tantalizing. In their family, food was always present to deal with a crisis.

"Mama, Mama!"

"Stop screamin' gal. I'm back here."

Sunny could smell the cleaning spray. Her mother was cleaning the bathroom. The one good thing about her mother's visit, her house would be spotless when she left.

Sunny hugged her mother casually, and went to her room. Setting down the bag her mother brought to the hospital, she stepped out of her shoes, and into a pair of fuzzy slippers.

Padding back up the hall she heard her mother say, "Pick up ya feet."

"Do you want some tea Mama?"

"Yes, thank ya."

Sunny put the kettle on the stove, simply buying time. It whistled, and her mother walked into the kitchen. As Sunny fixed the cups, her mother asked the question she wanted to ask at the hospital, but wouldn't.

"Did ya inten' to kill yosef?"

Sunny sighed, but didn't say anything.

"Answer me gal."

"No, I didn't. My intention was to get Grant's attention. Now, I said it. You satisfied?"

"No matter if I'm satisfied. Ya really are crazy, an' ya need to be in that psych ward. How did that work out for ya?"

"Mama, I cannot wrap my head around Grant just flippin' the script on me, and marrying some girl he met two months ago. He's the insane one. Or her for marryin' him!"

"I don disagree wit you, but that's what happened. But be clear he didn't flip no script. That man plainly told ya he wouldn' marry ya because ya kept lyin' and decivin' him. Sunny ya brought that on yosef."

"Mama, you have made your disgust with me, and my handling this relationship with Grant clear. You don't have to say anything else."

"Good, so pack yo things, prepare to sell this house. Ya need to move back home. Ya need supervision."

Sunny laughed. "You must be kidding! I am not moving back to Eleuthera. I'm not leaving D.C."

"Do you think they gone keep ya at that hospital when they find out what ya tried to do? 'Specially wit him workin' there?"

"They can't fire me for that."

"Maybe not, but they can send ya to anotha place."

Sunny's mother was right, but Sunny hadn't considered all that. And, under the circumstances, she wouldn't put it pass Grant to request she be transferred. "Well I will just take my chances."

Sunny wasn't as confident as she pretended to be.

"Crazy gal. Ya betta stat lookin' fo anotha job."

In the midst of twisting and turning most of the night, Sunny decided to tell her friends she met another guy, and was moving away to be with him. As soon as she found a job, that's what she would do.

Chapter 56

"I'm glad you made it today April," the counselor said. "Family support is critical in these situations."

April smiled. "I love Lane, and I do want to support him in this."

As the counselor reviewed with Lane their prior session, April looked around the office. It was beyond immaculate. Absolutely nothing was out of place. There were framed certificates on the wall, and plaques and trophies on shelves. On one wall were her degrees; bachelors, two masters, Ph.D., PsyD. "Why does she need all those degrees?" April thought and tuned back in to what the counselor and Lane were discussing. The counselor made eye contact with April periodically, and engaged her in the conversation. April's assessment; Lane was right. She was a bit over the top. Her diction, her body language. She made sure you know who's the expert. But at the end of the session, April felt good that counseling was working for Lane. The additional take away, they needed to have Pre-Martial counseling. They hadn't talked about it, or really even considered it.

"What's up baby sis?" Ben said answering April's call.

"Lane and I are making wedding plans, and it occurred to us we didn't have Pre-Martial counseling on the schedule or in the plans."

"Let me assure you it was on my radar, but I'm glad you called."

They talked and made the first two of six appointments.

"He is emailing us some homework."

"Homework?" Lane looked at April sideways.

"You have a problem with homework?"

Lane sighed, "Actually yeah. You know I don't know much about my family. I don't know who my dad is. I hate answering a bunch of personal questions."

April didn't respond immediately. The counselor had asked Lane if there were things in his past that may be contributing to his binges, and he said no. But there it was. His insecurities about his family background. "Babe, Ben doesn't know who his daddy is either, so he will definitely be able to relate to you about that." Lane's countenance changed. April kept talking. "Remember I told you his mom was killed in an accident…"

…caused by Belinda's mom. Yeah I remember…"

…your situation won't be challenging to him." April said.

Lane felt better on the surface, but deep down he was fearful of the questions he would have to answer.

"Did you and Tamara have marriage counseling? April asked Lane.

He chuckled. "If that's what you want to call it. Her cousin performed the ceremony. We met with him twice, once for counseling and once to talk about the ceremony."

"Did he say anything useful?" April looked at Lane puzzled.

"He basically said take the vows seriously, and don't go to bed angry at each other. Except he quoted the actual scripture."

"That's good advice," April said smiling.

"Yeah, but Tam and I went to bed angry many nights."

"Did you love her? I mean, I know you loved her, but were you heart broken when the marriage ended?"

"April where is all this coming from?"

"Everything you've said about your marriage to Tamara has been negative, yet you two were together for years. There had to be some good in it."

Lane exhaled loudly, deeply. "I loved Tam, but not like I love you. With her it was a needy kind of love. I needed her to love me, or so I thought. She was 'somebody' and I was nobody. To answer your question; by the time we physically separated I was numb. I was heartbroken when I found out she lied about being on birth control. My love for you is different, better, deeper. You give me strength. You make me better. You love me as much as I love you, and I know it, I feel it."

April closed her eyes, and let the tears she was fighting roll down her cheeks. She hurt for Lane because she loved him, and didn't want anything or anybody to hurt him again. "I love you too," she whispered. "I promise to always be there for you, and know that you make me stronger too."

"We're good for each other," he said.

Chapter 57

Carissa and Sterling held hands walking into the lobby of the women's center. Sterling wore jeans, boots and a sweater. The look was different because he wore sweat suits most of the time. Carissa wore a jumpsuit, blazer, high heel pumps and the diamond ring Sterling gave her a few days before. She hadn't agreed to marry him, but was wearing the ring. She wanted to know what he did with Kathy's ring.

"I sold it back to the jeweler."

All Carissa really cared about was the ring he gave her wasn't the same ring.

They were early on purpose. Sterling wanted to see the look on Kathy's face when she saw Carissa. Kathy didn't disappoint. She gasped, and was totally tongue tied. Her reaction wasn't lost on Carissa either. She knew this was the determining factor; if Kathy intended to re-establish her relationship with Sterling. This was the moment this whole arrangement was designed for. The reason Sterling asked her to be in his life. The problem, she was falling for him, and he was falling for her too. Carissa had to decide quickly if she would be a bitch or very sweet to Kathy.

Sterling made the introductions. Katherine was with Kathy. "How are you Carissa? I don't know if you remember, but we've met before."

"Yes, I do remember Mrs. Robinson. I'm well. How are you?"

Carissa's smile was beautiful, Kathy thought, and she felt fat and underdressed. Sterling wanted to touch Kathy's baby bump, but he didn't, for Carissa, but also because he didn't want to do anything emotional toward Kathy, who was obviously shocked.

"Kathy you should check in," Katherine said.

Kathy walked away, and was glad for the minute away from the others.

"Would you like to have a seat Mrs. Robinson?"

"Thank you," Katherine said sitting. Carissa sat too. Sterling remained standing until Kathy came back and sat down. He sat between Carissa and Katherine. While they waited, he asked Kathy several questions, about the pregnancy. She answered, keeping her eyes on Carissa's expression.

"Pregnancy agrees with you Kathy. Your hair and skin are beautiful," Carissa said to her.

"Thanks," Kathy's reply was dry.

"Sterling and I are excited about the baby. Of course he consistently says, 'he'..."

"It's a boy. I'm sure about that!"

Before Kathy or her mom could respond, the nurse called Kathy's name. All four of them stood.
"Let me get you set up, and I'll come back to get your family," the nurse said very kindly.

Kathy nodded, but didn't look back.

"We can't agree on a name either." Carissa said. Sterling wanted to laugh. Carissa was pushing all of Katherine's buttons. He was glad she was on his side!

Katherine addressed Sterling not responding to Carissa's comments. "What are you doing?"

"What do you mean?" Sterling looked puzzled because he genuinely was.

"Why is Carissa here, and why is she talking like she has anything to do with any of this?"

"Mrs. R, she has everything to do with this. She and I will be his parents." On cue Carissa raised her left hand and wiggled her fingers. Katherine didn't respond to the gesture, but addressed Sterling again.

"How is that even possible when three months ago you proposed to Kathy?"

"Who been real straight, she don't want me or my kid!"

That comment hurt Katherine, whose next remark was addressed to Carissa. "And how can you consider a future with a man you barely know? Obviously you're his rebound." Her whisper was forceful.

Carissa smiled. "As an athlete Mrs. Robinson I can tell you, games can be won on rebounds."
Sterling resisted the urge to fist bump Carissa. Katherine rolled her eyes at Carissa. She was furious. Her plan hadn't materialized, and now Sterling had gone to plan B. He had changed. He wasn't the same guy who agreed with her that Kathy needed to come home.

"You all may come on back." The nurse said to the three of them.
"Carissa doesn't need to join us," Katherine said.

Neither Carissa nor Sterling commented, they just followed the nurse through the door and down the hall. Sterling was nervous. He was borderline emotional about seeing the baby, coupled with Kathy's indifference. But he was grateful Carissa was there. And he was right, the baby was a boy.

Chapter 58

"Damn! What time is it?" Lane rolled off the sofa. The sun was bright in the living room window. He squinted. It was so bright it hurt his eyes. He bumped his knee on the coffee table. Looking around there was an empty vodka bottle on the floor, a half empty bottle and a glass on the table. His head hurt and his stomach was queasy. "I should already be at the church," he thought looking at his watch. "April is going to think I left her at the altar." He staggered across the room, took a gulp of the liquor left in the glass, stumbled and fell.

The ringing phone startled Lane. He woke up in a cold sweat, his heart beating rapidly, and he was breathing hard. He looked around the room. He was in his bedroom. There was no vodka bottle. It was a dream. A bad dream. He looked over at April. She slept soundly. Lane eased out of bed, walked quietly downstairs and answered. After the call he went to the kitchen and started a cup of coffee. His hands trembled. The dream shook him to his core. "I gotta get some help," he thought. He pondered his options, stirring the coffee absent mindedly.

Kissing April on her cheek. Lane also rubbed her back. "Wake up baby." She turned over, blinking to focus her eyes. "I'm sorry to wake you, but I need your help." He told her about the dream. His voice cracking, and tears in his eyes. "I don't know what to do. I need help."

April sat up, but didn't say anything for a few moments. Lane sat quietly and waited. She took the coffee cup from his hand, took a sip, thinking "what have I gotten myself into?"

As if reading her mind, Lane said, "please don't leave me April."

"Baby you know better," she said. "I love you."

Lane's shoulders relaxed a little. April glanced at the clock, it wasn't even eight o'clock yet.

"We'll call the counselor in a few minutes to see what she suggests."

He nodded. She put her arms around him, and kissed him hard. He needed to go back to sleep so she could think. April climbed onto Lane's lap. He responded. She knew he would. A little while later he was sleeping, and April was downstairs making coffee.

April called Belinda. Knowing there was a great possibility of interruption, she got right to the point.

"He's asking for help. He's not hiding the problem. You have to honor and respond to that," her sister advised.

"He's going to counseling. I don't know what else to do."

Belinda sighed. "April if you are afraid to marry Lane for fear the drinking may not be under control, then you have to tell him that and call it off."

"I'll call you back. I hear him coming down the steps," April said and hung up.

"So that's how you do a brother? Knock me out, and leave me in the bed alone?" He stretched and April saw he wore only gym shorts. Walking behind her Lane put his arms around April and held her tightly, then kissed her shoulders. "Come over here for a minute," he took her hand and they sat at the table in the breakfast nook. "I want to call the counselor, but I am going to tell her I need more intense counseling. Something other than talking to her."

"Maybe you need a male counselor, or you need to go to A.A.," April said.

"A.A. wouldn't be different, just more people in the room with the same problem," he said.

April's phone rang. It was Ben. "I know we're not scheduled to meet today, but I think we should." He continued without waiting for April to reply.

"Okay, what time?"

Disconnecting the call, April told Lane about the conversation with Belinda, which she knew prompted the call from Ben.

"Are you fearful of being my wife April?"

"No, but I am fearful of losing you to something neither of us can see coming."

Chapter 59

The broadest grin ever was on Sterling's face, as the ultrasound tech moved the wand across Kathy's belly. "He's a pretty big boy" the doctor said. Carissa's hand rested on Sterling's back. He, Katherine and Kathy were doing most of the talking. She was lost in her own thoughts.

"I hope I am pregnant now. He is smitten with this baby. What if Kathy changes her mind now?" Carissa's mind raced from one thought to another. When she zeroed back to the conversation in the room, the nurse was wiping the gel off Kathy's stomach, and asking them to leave.

"Sterling can you wait a minute?" Kathy asked.

"Yep," he responded. Carissa's heart skipped a beat, but she walked out in front of Katherine.

In the waiting room, Katherine continued with her inquisition of Carissa, who refused to back down. "Mrs. Robinson with all due respect, I am a fact of your life you need to get used to." Before Katherine could snap back her phone rang. It was Lee. She moved away from Carissa to talk privately. Carissa was glad, but the debate with

Katherine had taken her mind off Sterling and Kathy for a few minutes.

"Thanks for coming," Kathy said.

"I wouldn't miss seeing my boy for the first time," Sterling was still smiling.

"What is the nature of your relationship with Carissa? Obviously she's here so it must be serious."

"Yes, it's serious," he said. Kathy swallowed hard. "She's excited about the baby too! I told her it would be a boy!" Kathy watched Sterling's body language. He was thrilled about this baby. Kathy wished she felt the same way.

"Sterling I'm glad you and Carissa are happy. That means he will be happy too." She took a deep breath, and continued talking. Can we write an agreement for custody and visitation? And I will pay you child support when I get out of school."

"I already discussed all this with a lawyer. She's gonna send you the papers to review."

"Sterling why do we need to involve a lawyer?"

"'Cause I don't want to beef with your parents, or you coming back later trying to reverse things. And, I need to protect Carissa if anything happens to me."

"You plan to marry her Sterling?"

"You didn't notice the ring?"

"No, I didn't. That's awfully fast," Kathy said with a little attitude.

"Why you care? You gave me yo ass to kiss." Even as he was talking Sterling didn't know what he would say if Kathy said she wanted him back.

"No I didn't. I was very honest with you, about the baby, and now I'm trying to make sure he's taken care of."

"Honest? Is that why you accepted my proposal, knowing you had no intention of marrying me?"

Kathy had no rebuttal. She told Sterling she would be on the lookout for the papers from his lawyer, and asked him to leave the room.

Closing the door behind him, Sterling exhaled. He had held that air in his lungs for as long as he and Kathy were alone. One thing he knew for sure, he wanted and needed Carissa. He needed her energy, her understanding, her reasoning, her love. She loved him, and Kathy didn't. She wanted him and his son. Kathy did not. If Kathy ran to the door and declared her undying love for him, and screamed to the top of her lungs she wanted him back, he would say no. He would walk away. He knew that now, and he had to make sure Carissa knew it. Holding the door to the waiting room for the nurse and another patient, Sterling looked in. He saw Katherine by the window with her back turned. He couldn't see Carissa until he was in the room. Not saying anything he grabbed her hand, and walked out.

Kathy dressed slowly. She could only blame herself for how she was feeling. This was the cost of freedom, independence and career over family. Knowing her parents were thoroughly disappointed didn't help either. Deep inside Kathy knew this was right for her, and for her son.

"A boy," Kathy said aloud, Sterling said it would be." She felt sad. She had not bonded with the baby. Kathy was eating properly, resting, going for walks, taking her vitamins; all the things she should do to give birth to a healthy baby. But, she hadn't given any serious thought to a name or any of the other preliminary things expectant mothers did. She had wondered how surrogate mothers could carry babies and then give them away. Now she understood.

Her thoughts were interrupted by her phone. At a glance she needed to answer. The caller identified herself, as the person who wanted to sub-lease Kathy's apartment for the summer. "I will be leaving the second week in May, and back mid-August," Kathy sighed as she explained to her. They worked out some details, and ended the call. Kathy was grateful not to have the conversation in her mother's presence. All she wanted was to get through these next few months and get back to the life she wanted.

In the parking lot, Kathy noticed Sterling open the car door for Carissa. She felt a tug at her heart strings. As she and Katherine drove out of the parking lot, Carissa and Sterling were still sitting in the car.

"Thank you love."

"For what?" Carissa asked.

"For being my ride or die. For having my back in the middle of all this shit."

"I am a woman of my word Sterling. When you asked me to play this role, I committed to an award winning performance."

"Are you still playing?"

Carissa was caught off guard by the question. She took a moment to regroup before she answered him. "No, actually I'm not playing. Not anymore. The acting was over the first night I spent in your arms. What I've known and wanted for twenty plus years became my reality." Carissa's tone of voice suddenly changed. "Why, where are we going with this Sterling?"

"Whoa! Hold up! We not going anywhere with this. Real talk; I 'preciate you."

"You're welcome," she said softly.

"In case you have any concerns, Kathy is out of the picture."

"Her choice or yours?"

"She didn't say anything different, but if she had it didn't matter, I'm done. I want you. My boy and I need you in our lives."

They were both quiet for a moment. Carissa broke the silence, "Yes, Sterling. I will marry you."

Chapter 60

Lane and April arrived at the church, expecting only Ben to be there, but surprisingly there was another car. Inside they saw Belinda, chatting with a lady they recognized as a member of the church, but not someone they really knew.

A few moments later Ben and another gentleman came down the hall. He asked the group to join him in the conference room. Making the introductions, Ben knew Lane was puzzled, but he wanted to do this right. Finally, Ben introduced them to Nathan.

"Lane, I want you to hear what Nathan has to say." Lane nodded. April took his hand and they sat on a love seat, both completely and obviously baffled about what was coming next. April looked at Belinda for some comfort. Her face was non-descript.

"Son, first let me say you among friends. My Mrs., and I been whey you at. Only diffrance, we was aready married wit a baby comin'. I was drankin' too much. Workin' eryday. Thought she was gone leave me. I kept 'pologizing, but didn't stop." Nathan's wife nodded in agreement, with a pleasant smile on her face. He kept talking. "Wife axed me ta drive 'er ta chuch on a Sunday evenin.' I was in fronta the tv, watchin' football, wit no plan a goin' nowhere." He chuckled. "But she was 'specting so I took 'er. Got there she tells me she signed me up ta get baptized!" They both laughed. When I start ta protess, she told me frankly I needed ta stop drankin' and she believed gettin' baptized would hep me. What I know now was the Spirit, but it was like somethin' said in my ear, 'do it.' I got baptized that day, and ain't took a drank sents."

April's heart rate had slowed back to normal. She knew what Ben was planning, and she was perfectly fine with it. Lane on the other hand; not so much. Lane started attending Landridge Community Church after he started courting April. He joined after their relationship got serious. Unlike April, he hadn't grown up in church, and even as an adult he had not decided to be baptized. But now, Lane found himself faced with a decision; either way it would change his life.

"I know this is a lot to process Lane," Ben said.

"Yeah," was all Lane could say.

"For the good of your life with April, but more importantly for your own peace of mind, I want you to seriously consider being baptized."

"Son, you kin leave all that drankin' in the water, come up clean, sober, able ta move on," Nathan said. His wife made eye contact with April, smiled and nodded.

April squeezed Lane's hand. She whispered, "I think it's a good idea. This thing is haunting you. I agree that only God can heal you.

Not responding Lane walked across the room and looked out the window. The room was quiet; all eyes were on him except Ben's. His eyes were closed. He was praying. April started to get out of her seat, but Nathan's wife shook her head "No". The wail startled everyone in the room. It was Lane, overcome with raw emotion. After a few moments of allowing him to get it out, Nathan went to him, and with a hand on his shoulder led Lane out of the room. Ben followed. April was crying too, but she stayed put.

After a few minutes, Ben came back and asked the ladies to join them in the sanctuary. A few more minutes passed and Ben appeared in the window behind the choir area. Standing in the baptism pool, he reached forward, and Lane descended the few steps into the water. Nathan was standing on the steps opposite Lane. After a moment he stepped into the water too. April stood in the middle, Nathan's wife on one side, Belinda on the other. The three of them held hands. They couldn't hear what Ben said to Lane, but they could see both of them chuckle slightly. Then with Nathan's assistance, three dips into the water. He stood only a few seconds, and then disappeared up the steps. He could be heard sobbing. April unclasped the other ladies' hands, and sat holding her head in both hands. She sobbed too.

After the baptism, Lane, Ben and Nathan had a long talk and Nathan promised Lane he would help him through the "aftermath."

"Thangs gone change. Be harda some days than others, but you kin do it."

Chapter 61

Sterling Emerson Chance, II was born a few weeks early, but perfectly healthy. Kathy's blood pressure had been higher than normal, and the doctor recommended inducing labor. Kathy's parents tried again unsuccessfully to talk her out of giving the baby to Sterling and Carissa. The hospital psychologists and a nurse talked Kathy into pumping her breast milk for a few weeks. The gesture was more of an emotional attachment than she wanted. Listening to the counselor, Kathy agreed, for the health of the baby. "The baby" was how she referred to him, not wanting to get too familiar with the child.

Sterling cried when the nurse laid his son in his arms. For a few minutes, he just held him, and stared. While the nurse cleaned him up, Sterling went to get Carissa. She entered the suite, but stayed on the side of the curtain where she couldn't see Kathy. Sterling stepped around the drape and placed the bundle in Carissa's arms.

"Hi Deuce", she whispered, and kissed his forehead. She and Sterling decided on the nickname for him. Snapping a couple of pictures with his phone, he took the baby out of Carissa's arms, kissed her lips, and disappeared behind the curtain again. Carissa went back to the waiting room. Her smile wasn't lost on Katherine and Lee.

Katherine would take the secret she and Sterling shared to her grave, and would regret it forever. She wanted her daughter to be a wife and mother, not more attached to a career. When Sterling pricked the condom and Kathy got pregnant, Katherine thought it was a done deal. Nothing could be farther from the truth.

When Katherine and Lee went in to see Deuce, Sterling went to the waiting area. His long hug with Carissa was interrupted by a lady with a laptop computer on a portable stand. She explained her job was to register the baby's birth certificate. Sterling answered her questions. The lady printed the document she typed, and gave it to him on a clip board. He signed, and gave the document to Carissa. In the section that said adoptive parent, she checked the box for mother, and signed her name; Carissa Jade Chance. Handing the clip board back to the lady, she twirled the diamond wedding band around her finger.

Chapter 62

Lane followed Ben into the sanctuary. The smile on his face was infectious. He was sharp in the white dinner jacket, and dress shoes with no socks. April loved that look. He glanced at the baptism pool just for a moment. He would be forever grateful for that pool. It held the answer to the residue of his adult life.

A few minutes later Brittani came down the aisle, then Brianna, both looking very grown up in the identical tangerine dresses, and pearls. When April came down the aisle on Hampton's arm, Lane released an audible gasp. He, at that moment, fell in love with her all over again.

The wedding and reception were everything April wanted, and none of what she didn't; in spite of the twins' protests.

When April laid her head on Lane's shoulder, and closed her eyes, he laid his head on her head, and closed his eyes too. Just as he exhaled the airplane lifted off the ground. "Next stop, ten days of sun, fun, food, and sex," he thought, "but no alcohol."

Other Books By Cheryl McCullough

The Wedding Party

Absent…One From Another

Christmas Dinner

www.ingramcontent.com/pod-product-compliance
Lightning Source LLC
Chambersburg PA
CBHW071352290426
44108CB00014B/1510